GLOBAL VOICES
for Gender Justice

Ramathate T.H. Dolamo,
Ana Maria Tepedino, and
Dwight N. Hopkins, co-editors

Wipf & Stock
PUBLISHERS
Eugene, Oregon

Wipf and Stock Publishers
199 W 8th Ave, Suite 3
Eugene, OR 97401

Global Voices for Gender Justice
Edited by Dolamo, Ramathate T. H., Tepedino, Ana Maria, and Hopkins, Dwight N.
Copyright©2001 by Hopkins, Dwight N.
ISBN 13: 978-1-55635-646-9
ISBN 10: 1-55635-646-3
Publication date 10/2/2007
Previously published by The Pilgrim Press, 2001

Contents

Introduction	*Dwight N. Hopkins*	7
The Labour of Compassion: Voices of "Churched" Korean American Women	*Jung Ha Kim*	9
"A New Black Heterosexual Male"	*Dwight N. Hopkins*	25
The Gendered Forms of Racism: A Native American Woman's Perspective	*Andrea Smith*	43
Latin American Feminist Theology and Gender Theories	*Silvia Regina de Lima Silva*	62
Culture/Gender in Latin America	*Diego Irarrazaval*	72
Gender and New (Re-newed) Images of the Divine	*Ana Maria Tepedino*	84
The Shifting Gender Role of Women	*Judith Na Bik Gwat*	97

Harmonizing Masculine and Feminine in the Male Gender	*Oswald B. Firth*	111
Gender Concern – A Male Perspective in Wholistic Paradigm	*J.B. Banawirmata*	129
The Portrait of Women in the Parables	*Kemdirim O. Protus*	139
A Critical Review of Cheryl Exum's Feminist Interpretation of Hebrew Canon Patriarchy	*Ramathate T.H. Dolamo*	152
Gender Mainstreaming In African Theology: An African Woman's Perspective	*Philomena N. Mwaura*	165

Contributors

Jung-Ha Kim teaches in the sociology department of Georgia State University and is a member of the EATWOT U.S.A. minorities.

Dwight N. Hopkins teaches theology at the University of Chicago Divinity School (U.S.A.). He is the coordinator of the EATWOT Theological Commission. Some of his books are *Introducing Black Theology of Liberation* and *Heart and Head: black theology past, present, and future.*

Andrea Lee Smith is a member of the EATWOT U.S.A. minorities. A Native American scholar and activist, she is affiliated with the University of California at Santa Cruz.

Silvia Regina de Lima Silva is a member of EATWOT from Brazil who teaches at the Universidad Biblica Latinoamerica in San Jose, Costa Rica.

Diego Irarrazaval is the vice-president of EATWOT. Director of the Institute for Aymaran Studies and associate pastor of Parroquia de Chucuito (in Puno, Peru), his latest book is *Inculturation: new dawn of the church in Latin America.*

Ana Maria Tepedino is a member of the EATWOT theological commission and is from Rio de Janeiero, Brazil.

Judith Na Bik Gwat is an EATWOT member from Indonesia.

Oswald B. Firth, OMI is a member of EATWOT and is attached to the Centre for Society and Religion in Sri Lanka.

J.B. Banawiratma, SJ is a member of the EATWOT theological commission and is on the faculty of theology at Sanata Dharma University in Indonesia. His book is *Contextual Social Theology: an Indonesian Model.*

Kemdirim O. Protus, an EATWOT member from Africa, teaches in the Department of ReligiousStudies at the University of Port Harcourt, Nigeria.

Ramathate T.H. Dolamo is a member of the EATWOT theological commission and teaches theological ethics at the University of the North in Pietersburg, South Africa.

Philomena N. Mwaura teaches at Kenyatta University (Kenya) and writes on topics of gender, African Instituted Churches, and religious studies. She is a member of EATWOT.

Gender: Voices from the Third World
Introduction by Dwight N. Hopkins

Gender is usually associated with creative conversations among female scholars, activists, and church leaders, thus leaving out the investigation of this concept and reality from a male's perspective. Similarly, we note the rise of feminist thought particularly in North America and, therefore, an emphasis on the experiences of middle and upper income white women. In this instance, Third World women (from Africa, Asia, the Caribbean, Latin America, the Pacific Islands, and U.S. minorities) have mainly been disregarded or offered as tokens in the discussions. And too often in the gender divide between men and women, there has been more ignoring or castigating than conversation, especially from the stance of arrogant or defensive men.

What is required is an examination of gender that takes seriously the often silenced voices of Third World women while, at the same time, incorporating the input of Third World men. More specifically, there needs to be an engagement between male and female genders both of whom undergo additional and layered occurrences of race, ethnicity, class, sexual orientation, and post-colonial national developments in the Third World. What does faith have to do with the multiplicity and multi-dimensionality of these challenges?

Gender: Voices from the Third World seeks to initiate an intentional reflection to facilitate the filling of this void by offering constructive statements on the nature of gender in the lived contexts of Third World women and men. This volume results mainly from essays prepared for a global gathering of members of the international Theological Commission of the Ecumenical Association of Third World Theologians (EATWOT).[1] The Association began in 1976 and, subsequently, has developed into the only worldwide network of liberation theologians from the majority of the land bases on the earth.[2] Though primarily constituted by lay workers, pastors, and scholars from the developing countries, EATWOT also includes limited membership from United States minorities (that is African Americans or blacks, Asian Americans, Hispanics or Latinos/as, and Native Americans or American Indians).

Comprised of delegates from Africa, Asia, Latin America, U.S. minorities, and the executive committee of EATWOT, the Theological

Commission meeting (from which this is the result) took place in the new South Africa whose constitutional policy explicitly advocates the creation of a non-sexist, post-apartheid government and society. Consequently, such a favorable disposition toward gender equality on the part of the new democratic government and progressive young country proved to be a very encouraging environment for debating and affirming the visioning of novel and healthy gender social interactions. In a word, the first international assembly of females and males on the question of gender relations forged a fresh path in the midst of the latest post colonial, independent government in the Third World.

The following questions, among others, motivate this book. How does the abstract notion of gender reveal itself in the practicality of diverse cultures, contexts, and communication modes? What roles do tradition, genealogy, and history play relative to modernity and contemporary political and economic issues? What is the difference between sex and gender? And, fundamentally, where does faith commitments fit into all of these pressing issues?

Gender: Voices from the Third World breaks new ground with the introduction of men and women of faith both sharing on the essential and dynamic characteristics of the gendered humanity. If we are all made in the image of an ultimate spirituality of genuine interaction between females and males based on equality, justice, the sanctity of the human person, and service to the least among us (on a global scale this underscores especially the disproportionate plight of women and children), then what has skewed the original intent of a shared community?

Notes

1. This Theological Commission meeting took place July 28th through the 31st, 2000 at the Willowpark Conference Centre in Johannesburg, South Africa. At that time, I was coordinator of the Theological Commission.

2. The Association arose out the commonalities of life experienced by Christians and justice minded people in the developing world; hence the only land base not officially represented is Europe. For information on the formation of EATWOT, see Oscar K. Binwenyi, "A l'origine de l'association oecumenique des theologiens du tiers monde," in *Bulletin de Theologie Aricane* 2, no. 3 (January-June 1980); James H. Cone, "Ecumenical Association of Third World Theologians," Ecumenical Trends 14, no. 8 (September 1985); Sergio Torres, "Dar es Salaam 1976,' in Theologies of the Third World: Convergences and Differences, ed. Leonardo Boff and Virgil Elizondo (Edinburgh: T. And T. Clark, 1988), 105-15; and Dwight N. Hopkins, Introducing Black Theology of Liberation (Maryknoll, New York: Orbis Books, 1999), chapter 5.

The Labour of Compassion: Voices of "Churched" Korean American Women

Jung Ha Kim

When Chinese come to the United States, they start laundromats and Chinese restaurants; when Japanese come to the United States, they start business corporations; when Koreans come to the United States, they start their churches.

This overgeneralized and ethnocentric remark about Asian Americans actually reveals at least one significant socio-cultural fact about Korean Americans: their church growth.[1] The traditional formula for estimating the Korean American population in a given area – the number of Korean American churches in the area multiply by 500[2] - reflects an astonishing and distinct characteristic of the highly "churched" Korean American population in the United States. Sociologists and theologians agree that over 70 percent of Korean Americans are said to be self-claimed Christians compared to only 13 percent of the total population in South Korea in 1982, and 18-21 percent since 1986.[3] Such a dramatic increase of the "churched" population among Korean Americans living in the U.S. may be attributed to the peculiar mission of Korean American churches. On the one hand, they offer a vehicle for "Americanization"; and on the other hand, they provide sites for Korean cultural preservation and elaboration.

Conspicuously absent in the thesis of Christianization in either the Americanization or Koreanization process is a focus on Korean women's participation in the church, even as women constitute a majority of its attendees across states. In fact, the so-called Christianization of Korean Americans is predominantly a feminization of church attendees.

Ironically, the study of "churched" Korean American women has been hindered by their shared membership with more conspicuous "minority" groups, namely Korean American men, with whom they share race-ethnicity, and other women of color, with whom they share a gender identity. As a result, scholars tend to overlook Korean American women's experiences by assuming that their realities are identical to those of Korean American men and/or other women of color.[4] Furthermore, although an increasing number of writers have addressed themselves to the Korean American church – its numerical growth, its schisms, and its multifarious functions – no one has focused specifically on women's experiences in a systematic way.[5] No published studies of the Korean American church have ever considered the church experience within a gendered context. This initial study addresses the following questions: given that the Christian church is both patriarchal and potentially liberatory, and given that the Korean American church is supposed to minister to its members in multiple ways as a racial-ethnic institution within dominant culture(s), how do Korean American women experience their church? In particular, how does patriarchy operate within a Korean American church? How do Korean American women's hyphenated identities become socially and religiously organized? Is it possible to find a sense of "home" in an institution through investigation of and inquiry into one's experiences of being a woman within the Korean American church context?

In order to address the foregoing questions I utilized participant observations, in-depth interviews, oral histories, and written historical documents. Moreover, these research methods were instrumental for placing "churched" Korean American women's experiences and their own articulations at the center of this exploratory study. As a qualitative attempt to examine the lives of "churched" Korean American women from the perspective of an "outsider within,"[6] a special bilingual sensitivity also encouraged women to speak about their own lives and in their own terms. For many "churched" Korean American women suffer from "the cult of 'perfect' language," which is a form of censorship based on racism, sexism, classism, and neocolonialism in the U.S.[7]

My work is also significantly influenced by "feminist" methodologies.[8] Feminist research adds an important vantage point of qualitative research by considering gender as a central organizing feature of peoples' lives and thus an important theoretical construct.

Participant observation and interviews were also enhanced by "woman-to-woman talk."[9] Woman-to-woman talk is often qualitatively different from talk in gender-mixed groups for at least two reasons: the woman listener is more likely to listen attentively and seriously and the woman speaker is more likely to use "language in non-standard ways"[10] for naming experiences. Woman-to-woman talk among racially-ethnically similar persons gives speakers an opportunity to describe their worlds with language perhaps not utilized by the dominant group(s) of the society.

The site chosen for the case study is the Kyo-whe (that is, the Korean word for church),[11] where I was a member and where I have served as a Director of Church Education (DCE) for the past four years.[12] It is situated in an upper-middle class neighbourhood of a large city in the Southeast part of the United States. The history of Kyo-whe formation and of its people are interrelated in that the first migration and immigration of the Korean Americans into the area (and to other parts of the Southern states) occurred after the

Immigration Act of 1965. Beginning with a few "pioneers" who came together to form the Kyo-whe in February of 1971 as one of the growing cadre of "new immigrants,"[13] the historical documentation of church directories demonstrate its steadily increasing membership: 49 households as of 1985, 68 as of October 1988, 85 as of November 1989 and 101 as of June 1990. The steady growth of the church has not occurred without turmoil, however, especially because of the schismatic tendency among the highly heterogeneous people who are its members. For instance, within the past twenty-four years, the church has gone through eleven different pastoral leaders. I recall three different pastoral leaders[14] in my own four years of serving the church.

Another difficulty for conducting a study of "living subjects" has to do with the differential alignment of power along lines of age, marital status, class and occupational prestige among adherents of the church and between the researcher and participants. My socio-religious status in the Kyo-whe is: unmarried (which can be translated as "not yet an adult" according to Korean tradition), non-ordained (often seen as "not as holy" as the ordained [male] ministers), relatively young (ageism is one of the powerful and typical ways to establish social relationships in Korean culture), and a church-related professional woman (that is, the Director of Church Education). Thus I do not fit easily into the traditionally understood category of church leader. Because of my non-traditional mixture of power and status, women of different status, prestige, and interests relate to me differently. And because of my official position in the church as DCE, I am keenly aware of the possibility that when women are asked to participate in informal interviews, they may be reluctant to deny my request. Questions arise, then, about whether the issue of standard informed consent is sufficiently voluntary. Hence, I was forced to come to terms with the realization that informed consent based on primary relationships is not a single contractual event, but an ongoing process.

In the larger research project, of which this essay is a part, I devoted considerable attention to substantiate the claim that the Korean American church is a deeply gendered and racially-ethnically identified institution whose material and ideological arrangements shape, facilitate, reinforce, and sometimes challenge "churched" Korean American women's construction of realities. To say that the church (or any other organization) is gendered means that "advantages and disadvantages, exploitation and control, action and emotion, meaning and identity, are patterned through and in terms of a distinction between male and female, masculine and feminine."[15] Insofar as these patterns systematically advantage males over females, it can be demonstrated that the church is a patriarchal institution.

With regard to material conditions, power structures within the church have typically excluded women from church leadership and religious authority. Women's ordination controversies,[16] differentiated dress codes, and the use of non-inclusive language to define and ritualize various transitional events in human life[17] can be cited as examples of women's exclusion from authority within the church. With regard to symbols and images, the Christian belief system represents a "culture"[18] that defines and justifies its members' gender biased world-view(s). Both the Old and the New Testaments of the Christian Bible are replete with calls for women's subordination (Ephesians 5:24), obedience (I Corinthians 14:33-35), and submission (Leviticus 8, 9, 12:1-5, 15, 18, and 21; and Ephesians 5:22) to men as the God-ordained (hence, "natural" and unquestionable) order. Thus, on the one hand, the Korean American church places men at the centre and behind the pulpit and women in the pews and kitchen-related areas, even as the latter constitutes the majority of church attendees in this patriarchal institution. At the same time, the very ethos and functions of the Korean American church are determined by the peculiar characteristics and needs of hyphenated people as its attendees; that is, both women and men blend their Korean and American realities.

A closer look at church history from a cross-cultural perspective, however, reveals that Christianity has the potential to be both oppressive and liberatory at the same time. That is to say, Christianity has been used as a powerful tool for legitimating the multifaceted oppression of non-Western countries around the world (especially the so-called "Third World"), for enslaving millions of African Americans, for colonizing (and neo-colonizing) the minds of "minority" groups, and for subordinating women globally. Christianity, however, also has been used as a powerful instrument for social change. With its preferential language for the poor and the oppressed (such as "the sermon on the mount"), the church liberated the lower and outcaste classes from illiteracy in Korea, mobilized the Civil Rights Movement of the late 1960s in the United States, provided the biblical roots and language for Latin Americans to articulate their liberation theologies, and empowered women's struggles to transform the patriarchal basis of Christianity. Hence, both the oppressive and liberating potential of the Christian church and its theologies are the context within which "churched" Korean American women find themselves.

At the same time, the Korean American church, as a racial-ethnic religious institution within a dominant culture, is the focal point of socio-cultural integration as well as the centre of community life for both its female and its male members. While providing ethnic homogeneity in a highly pluralistic society, the Korean American church not only serves as "mega church,"[19] with a variety of programs and specific interest groups – such as educating recent arrivals for simple, everyday survival skills like shopping, driving, job hunting, and finding an apartment – but also offers psychological and spiritual solace for its members.

In the context of this deeply gendered and highly race-ethnicity-conscious institution, "churched" Korean American women are aware of the fact that their own church rendered them to the secondary status and systematically excludes them from gaining public recognition. They are also aware that much of the church work is done by women, yet male church leaders tend to get the credit. As one woman in her mid-fifties aptly commented:

> Is there anything that doesn't require women's work in the church? [We both laughed at this remark.] I really think, all the work that is related to the church is, in fact, women's work. That most of the church work is done by women, but men tend to get all the credit. And I also think that that's just fine, because we women don't work for public recognition. If there are things that need to be done, then we [women] just do them. That's all.

In short, the Korean American church is a highly contradictory location where a presumably universal "gospel" is preached in a particular tongue, understood by people of hyphenated identities, and experienced through distinct socio-cultural lenses from various life circumstances. By juxtaposing patriarchal readings of the Christian "gospel" while beautifying and abstracting women's (especially, Korean mothers') suffering as the highest form of human love and Christian calling, the Korean American church preaches quasi-Christian messages in the name of religion. To put it differently, the Korean American church as a racial-ethnic institution provides "religious" explanations for its sexism and justifications for the pain experienced and pain endured in the lives of "churched" women. Furthermore, so long as "churched" Korean American women resist thinking of themselves as "100 percent American" and refuse to engage in collective amnesia of the culture they left behind, they are bound to feel an affinity toward the Koreanized Christian messages of women's suffering. "Churched" Korean American women, in turn, are called to sacrifice their interests and concerns as a gender group within their church, in order to reaffirm their sense of loyalty to racial-ethnic identities as a "minority" group within the United States.

However, by delving into both what "churched" Korean American women say and "listening around" to how they live everyday life in ways that they cannot articulate, I became convinced that they are highly gendered conscious and self-selected survivors. A peculiar set of handed-down folk wisdom and the "hidden transcripts" among women in the context of the Korean American church can demonstrate how they understand and articulate the seemingly oppressive experiences within their church:

> Men make rules in the house and in the church and we [women] follow them. [But] Making rules are not as difficult and self-sacrificial as trying to follow them.
>
> Korean men are bossy. They insist that they come first; they speak the last word; and they know better.
>
> Men think that they are the ones who take care of women, but in reality we take care of men. Men don't know anything about women.
>
> God created Korean women very strong. They can survive through anything.

"Churched" Korean American women's handed-down wisdom demonstrates that they use much of what is known as traditional language – such as "feminine", "deceptive," and "behind the scene" – to their own advantage. Why do "churched" Korean American women adhere to such seemingly oppressive gender roles and gender language within their church? Are they any advantages for women who insist on traditional understanding of gender? What are the costs? By asking these questions as another "churched" Korean American woman, I have encountered the much expected and neglected reality: the Korean American church exists as an important location for both resistance and liberation for women.

Lipman-Blueman called the utilization of "intelligence, canniness, intuition, interpersonal skills, charm, sexuality, deception, and avoidance"[20] as "micromanipulation," in order to offset the control of those more powerful.[21] That is to say, since women historically have had little access to publicly acknowledged power and control, they have learned to use what resources they do have to survive by utilizing informal means of influence.

"Churched" Korean American women also utilize extensive forms of nonverbal daily communication skills in the context of their church: frequent giggles, knowing glances, holding of hands, bitter similes, light hitting on arms, and constant eye contact. All these nonverbal forms of communication and articulated wisdom for survival can be seen as instrumental for fostering resistance and self-empowerment among "churched" Korean American women. James C. Scott calls both verbal and non-verbal forms of "critique of power spoken behind the back of the dominant" as a "hidden transcript."[22] For any subordinate groups, Scott argues "there is tremendous desire and will to express publicly what is the hidden transcript, even if that form of expression must use metaphors and allusions in the interest of safety."

Contrary to stereotypes, then, "churched" Korean American women are not all passive and victimized; indeed, they are social agents actively engaged in their own history-making. Racism, sexism, Americanization, Koreanization, Christianization, and the process of immigration have not defeated "churched" Korean American women in their ongoing struggle to maintain human dignity and give meanings to their everyday experiences in the United States. They take special pride in sharing with me how women have developed various strategies of micromanipulation and "hidden transcripts" within their church. "Churched" Korean American women also named their own struggles to be women, Koreans, Americans, and Christians all at the same time as the "labour of compassion." Rather paradoxically, however, in their articulations of "labour of compassion" within their church, women's understanding and experiences of silence is placed at the centre for achieving a sense of freedom, resistance, and liberation.

For instance, during the Sunday worship service, the predominantly female laity has no formal channel to raise their concerns, except through learned silence as a powerful symbol for both submission and for resistance. I am well aware of the fact that depending on the highly political decision as to how one conducts the study and/or constructs the reality, "churched" Korean American women's learned silence may signify internalized submission or self-conscious expression of resistance. Listening to how "churched" Korean American women speak about their own silence, however, has led me to conclude that their learned silence does not necessarily signify passivity or submission, but a form of resistance. For instance, as a woman in her later thirties said, "Sometimes it's better not to verbalize what I really feel and think. In that way [i.e., through silence], I can do whatever I choose to do without unnecessary arguments and headaches." Another woman in her late fifties offered more of a theological grounding for her learned silence: "Even in the doctrine of Trinity, the quiet power of the Holy Spirit plays an essential role of a mediator between God the Father and Christ the Son." Within the context of the Korean American church, then, silence is not to be interpreted solely as manifested subordination. For "silence as a will not to say or a will to unsay and as a language of its own"[23] has been understood and utilized by "churched" Korean American women as a powerful strategy for resistance.

Furthermore, in their seemingly docile silence, "churched" Korean American women nevertheless can learn to speak resistance in their own ways. They can express their deeply felt concerns through controlling their amounts of pledges to their church. Their very attendance at the church can also be utilized politically as a last resort to resist the minister's covert dominance over them. One woman in her mid-forties told me: "We [the women in the church] don't have much power in the church. But no one, not even the minister, can take away the power to withdraw from attending the church from us." In short, cultivating learned silence through knowing what not to say and when to keep quiet is often understood as a necessary growing experience for most "churched" Korean American women. One woman described what she means by "maturity" and "growing up as a woman" in the church:

Interviewee: "I hate some women in the church when they say 'I can't do this and that because I am a woman.' I think you just waste time asking men to do things for you. As you grow up, as a woman, you just have to know what to do."

Interviewer: "What do you mean? What are the things that women are supposed to know, you think?"

Interviewee: "As women, we are supposed to know when to keep quiet and when not to say anything."

Interviewer: "How do we know when to keep silent?"

Interviewee: (Looking at the interviewer with a puzzling smile) "You know. I'm sure you do. It [i.e., the knowledge] comes to us as naturally as menstruation."

Thus through their explicit display of subjugation by silence and submission, "churched" Korean American women have also learned to hold on to the "good" that lies in playing the traditionally expected gender roles. Rather ironically then, through their engineering of learned silence and embracing of traditional gender language and roles, "churched" Korean American women can experience both expected and unexpected rewards in their everyday lives. Furthermore, when "churched" Korean American women have experienced a certain social status and power through relationship to a successful and/or respected man over a good part of their lives, there is little reason for them to give up these traditional roles, especially without alternative avenues for achieving status and power in the U.S. Hence, when all is said and done, the "churched" Korean American women in my study pay little heed to the "women's freedom and liberation" talk of feminism of the dominant culture. In "this reversed world of human relationship in America," to borrow a "churched" woman's expression, the traditional gender roles and role expectations offer "churched" Korean American women alternative ways to be women.

If it is the case that "churched" Korean American women cultivate learned silence not merely as an act of submission, but also as a form of resistance and a survival strategy, then the claim that "breaking the silence" by the oppressed as the unquestionable key to liberation needs to be reexamined. The most viable survival and empowerment strategies of "churched" Korean American women must be understood in their own terms rather than through some presumably universal criterion for liberation. Perhaps not all attempts at liberation through micromanipulation are equally empowering, but they first must be understood in their own setting and evaluated within their own context. The prominent African American woman author, Alice Walker, writes in her much celebrated book, *The Color Purple*, that "it pisses God off if you walk by the color purple in a field somewhere and don't notice it."[24] And I dare say, I have seen the field of the color purple even in the context of the Korean American church.

Within this highly contradictory context of the Korean American church, my search was to elucidate various ways in which "churched" Korean American women find a sense of "home" (if they ever find it at all) in an institution within which their race-ethnicity is valued but their gender is devalued. What I learned from/with other "churched" Korean American women, through conducting this study, points to a clearly shared reality that they do not readily find a sense of "home" in their church; instead, through constant struggles they make a home for themselves. Together they strive to make a home mainly by utilizing "micromanipulative" survival skills and transmitting "hidden transcripts" from one woman to another, and one generation to the next. By refusing to be paralyzed by various forms of domination in their lives, they struggle to give meaning and names to self-identities and to dream of a better "home" for their U.S. born and raised descendants.

My study also points to the much neglected liberatory aspects of the Korean American church when women's experiences and self-understanding are placed at the center of the inquiry. Hence, the study reminds us about the importance of avoiding either/or constructions of reality. Both material and ideological dimensions intersect to produce both gender and racial and ethnic identification. The coercive and voluntaristic aspects of gender/racial-ethnic systems do not function as polar opposites either. Rather, they operate fluidly and complexly along the various intersections of everyday life so that "churched" Korean American women produce their gender, racial-ethnic, and religious identities in variable and complex ways from one life circumstance or social situation to another. Furthermore, "churched" Korean American women, as active social agents, have reaffirmed my own speculations about their hyphenated identities which reject neither the culture left behind nor the pressure to conform to the newly transplanted culture. The oppressive and liberatory aspects of participating in the church life do not function as polar opposite for "churched" Korean American women either. Rather they operate intricately and often simultaneously along various dimensions of everyday life. "Churched" Korean American women's lives are not played out as either victims of patriarchy or liberators from various oppressive systems, but as both. The "both-and" focus enables us to comprehend the richness and complexity of situated lives and thereby to do them justice.

Notes

1. This work was first presented at the "Women and Religion" session of the American Academy of Religion in 1992. The larger research project which this article is based on will be published as an Academy Series, "The Bridge-maker and Cross-bearers: Korean American Women and the Church" by Scholar's Press, 1996 (forthcoming).

2. From the mid-1980s, the formula was revised in the order to account for schisms producing a splitting/growing number of Korean Americans churches. The number of Korean American churches multiply by 380 or 400 (New York: The Christian Academy of New York, 1988); Y. Kim, "Church Growth: The Development of the Korean Church in America," Ph.D. dissertation, California Graduate School of Theology, 1990.

3. Jong Young Lee, "On Marginality: Toward an Asian American Theology," an unpublished presentation at the 1991 Annual meeting of the American Academy

of Religion in Kansas City, Kansas; Pyong Gap Min, "The Korean American Family," in *Ethnic Families in America: Patterns and Variations*, 3rd edition, edited by Charles H. Mindel, et. al. (New York: Elasevier, 1983); Eui Hang Shin and Hyun Park, "An Analysis of Causes of Schism in Ethnic Churches: the Case of Korean Americans Churches," *Sociological Analysis: A Journal of the Sociology of Religion* 49-3 (Fall, 1988), pp. 234-253.

4. Patricia Bell Scott and Gloria T. Hull, *Black Women in America: Social Science Perspectives* (Chicago: University of Chicago Press, 1989) discussed comparable problems for African American women. When race is discussed, audiences assume male gender, and when women are discussed, audiences assume white women.

5. Kyong-Suk Cho, "Korean Immigrants in Greham, Oregon: Community Life and Social Adjustment," an unpublished master's thesis, University of Oregon, 1963; Bong-youn Cho, "Korean Religions and Cultural Activities in the U.S." in *Koreans in America* (Chicago: Nelson Hall Press); Dae Gee Kim, *Major Factors Conditioning the Acculturation of Korean Americans with Respect to the Presbyterian in America and Its Ministry*, a Ph.D. dissertation in Missionology, Fuller Theological Seminary, 1985; Ilsoo Kim, *New Urban Immigrants: The Korean Community in New York* (Princeton: Princeton University Press, 1981); Won Moo Hurh, *Korean Immigrants in America: A Structural Analysis of Ethnic Confinement and Adhesive Adaptation* (Teaneck: Fairleigh Dickerson University Press, 1981); Shin and Park, "An Analysis and Causes of Schism in Ethnic Churches: the Case of Korean American Churches," *Sociological Analysis: A Journal of the Sociology of Religion* 49:3 (Fall 1988), pp. 234-253; David Kwan-sum Suh, *Korea Kaleidoscope: Oral Histories* (Sierra Mission Area, California: The Korean Oral History Project, United Presbyterian Church, 1983; Paul T. Kim, *Church Growth: The Development of the Korean Church in America*, Ph.D. dissertation, California Graduate School of Theology, 1984; Warren Y. Kim, *Koreans in America*, Seoul: Po Chin Chai, 1971; Eiu-young Yu, "Korean Communities in America: Past Present and Future," in *Amerasia Journal* 10 (1983), pp. 23-52.

6. Patricia Hill Collins, "Learning from the Outsider Within: The Sociological Significance of Black Feminist Thought," in *Social Problems* 33:6, pp. 114-32, December 1986; and Patricia Hill Collins, *Black Feminist Thought: Knowledge, Consciousness, the Politics of Empowerment*, Perspectives on Gender (Boston, Unwin Hyman, 1990).

7. Mitsuya Yamada, "The Cult of 'Perfect' Language: Censorship by Class, Gender and Race," a paper discussed at the Asian American Women's meeting in Englewood, New Jersey, September, 1992.

8. Judith Cook and Mary Margaret Fonow, "Knowledge and Women's Interests: Issues of Epistemology and Methodology in Feminist Sociological Research," *Sociological Inquiry* 56, 1 (Winter, 1986), p. 2-29; Judith Cook and Mary Margaret

Fonow (eds.), *Beyond Methodology: Feminist Scholarship as Lived Research* (Bloomington: Indianapolis: Indianapolis University Press, 1991); Helen Roberts (ed.), *Doing Feminist Research* (London: Routledge & Kegan Paul, 1981); and Sarah Matthews, "Rethinking Sociology through a Feminist Perspectives," *The American Sociologist* 17 (1982), pp. 29-35.

9. Dale Spencer, *Man Made Language* (London and Boston: Routledge and Kegan Paul, 1985); Marjorie DeVault, "Talking and Listening from Women's Standpoint: Feminist Strategies for Interviewing and Analysis," *Social Problems* 37:1 (February, 1990); and Clifford Geertz, *The Interpretation of Culture* (New York: Basic Books, Inc., 1973).

10. DeVault, p. 97.

11. The pseudonym, Kyo-whe, is a Korean word for the church.

12. Prior to making a decision about the research site, I was confronted by several ethical and methodological concerns. Although I did not accept the position of DCE four years ago from the Kyo-whe as an intentional "entrée into the field" (see Jorgensen, 1989; especially the section on "Entrée Strategies"), I felt that my commitment toward the church and a sense of personal integrity in dealing with various relationships within the church was at stake. I struggled with lingering questions – would the people perceive me as an opportunist, who uses/abuses human relationships in order to collect "data"? Would my relationships with people change because of my desire to do a case study of them? To what extent should I be overt/covert about the intentions, goals, and analyses of the study with the people? To what degree am I committed to being accountable to the people whom I study? Am I not living off less privileged people in order to gain access to the system of the more powerful? Would this study make any contribution(s) to the people, to the Korean American church, and to the larger community as a whole? What about the question of "objectivity" in this study? I decided to pursue the study largely based on two reasons: (1) my stance of "outsider within" (Collins, 1986, 1991) can provide a point of reference for understanding (*Verstehen* in the Weberian sense) the reality that is uncertain and unfamiliar from an outsider's perspective; and (2) most of my relationships with members of the Kyo-whe are built on solidarity from our commonly shared struggles as hyphenated people living in the U.S., and that basic trust between "fieldworkers and the hosts" (Wax, 1980:281) can enrich the quality of the data.

13. From an "insider's" perspective, perceiving Korean Americans as a "new immigrant" group is problematic. Although the "noticeable" number of Korean immigrants to the U.S. occurred after the 1965 Immigration Act, and the racial-ethnic category of "Korean" appeared for the first time in the U.S. Census in 1970, Korean Americans' history goes back to the year 1903. Hence, Korean

Americans who define the U.S. as their "homeland" need to reclaim their sense of "roots" from a distorted American history.

14. According to an article, "Methodists Keep Ministers Moving," in *The Atlanta Constitution*, June 30, 1990, the average stay of a Methodist minister at a church is three to four years.

15. Joan Acker, "Hierarchies, Jobs Bodies: A Theory of Gendered Organizations," *Gender and Society* 4:2 (June, 1990).

16. Katie G. Cannon, *Black Women Ethics* (Atlanta: Scholars Press, 1988); Mary Daly, *The Church and the Second Sex* (Boston: Beacon Press, 1968); Katie G. Cannon, *Beyond God the Father: Toward Philosophy of Women's Liberation* (Boston: Beacon Press, 1973); Carter Heyward, "The Power of God-with-us," *The Christian Century*, (March 14, 1990); and Meredith B. McGuirre, *Religion: The Social Context* (Belmont, California: Wadsworth Publishing Company, 1981).

17. Rosemary Radford Reuther, *Sexism and God-talk: Toward a Feminist Theology* (Boston: Beacon Press, 1983); and Pamela Dickey Young, *Feminist Theology/ Christian Theology* (Minneapolis: Fortress Press, 1990).

18. Geertz, p. 89.

19. Robert Wuthnow, *The Reconstruction of American Religion: Society and Faith Since World War II* (Princeton: Princeton University Press, 1988).

20. Jean Lipman-Blueman, *Gender Roles and Power* (Englewood Cliffs: Prentice-Hall, Inc., 1984).

21. Whereas socially legitimate and more visible control by the dominant group(s) is called "macro-manipulation."

22. James C. Scott, *Domination and the Arts of Resistance: Hidden Transcripts* (New Haven and London: Yale University Press, 1990), p. 164.

23. Trinh, T. Minh-ha, "Commitment from the Mirror-Writing Box," *Making Face, Making Soul: Creative and Critical Perspectives by Women of Color*, Gloria Anzaldua, ed., (San Francisco: an Aunt Lute Foundation Book, 1990), p. 373.

24. Alice Walker, *The Color Purple*, (New York: Washington Square Press, 1982), p. 178.

"A New Black Heterosexual Male"

Dwight N. Hopkins

Too many people within the African American community, church, and black theology in the United States believe that gender concerns only women. When the gender issue becomes the center of discussion, most black men, for example, assume a position as if they were corpses in a morgue. Their tongues grow silent; their bodies drop to a limp posture; and their lives fade into a ghost-like absence. Gender, from this vantage point, relates only to black women. If this logic is true, then it would be another example of black male sexism to enter the conversation and dominate what is said and not said. The flip side of this belief is that African American men do not have a gender. In contrast to this false view of life, this essay offers an interpretation of what it means to be, have, and live out a new heterosexual black male gender.[1] Black men have a gender. We have a male gender; so gender refers to men and women.[2]

Gender, in this essay, differs from sex and, therefore, opposes the popular idea of gender which makes sex and gender the same. However, in fact, sex speaks to human biology, the genitalia with which each person is born, while gender is defined and determined not by nature but by human culture. Usually, sex cannot be changed by human nurturing. Yet, gender construction remains a socialization process influenced by child rearing and parenting models, peer pressure and positive examples, movies and the media, educational institutions and training organizations, and biblical interpretation and faith communities. Human beings make other human beings into specific male and female genders. On the other hand, nature creates each person with the physical characteristics of a sex.[3] Sex exists as a biological category including reproductive capabilities, specific biological organs, and certain chemical balances. Sex is a neutral existence at birth; we are given our sex definitions when we come into the world; we do not define it at the point of birth delivery.

Restated, gender represents both a cultural category and a dynamic process of socialization. Culture includes a total way of life; that is, every aspect of a person's way of believing, thinking, judging, saying, and doing in the world. Culture, moreover, indicates a communal existence. There are no cultures of individuals, only cultures of people, groups, and communities.[4] As a result, we identify an individual based on his or her relation to and interaction with a group. Group culture contains certain rituals and myths which glue the culture together and help to distinguish one type of culture from another. Furthermore, culture always carries a specific language spoken by a group.

As a process of socialization, gender is not formed overnight, nor is it ever a completely finished product. As a vibrant creation, gender follows the ongoing formation of a culture. It changes in the sense that cultures of groups do not remain static. In the process of cultures modifying themselves continually, cultures also modify the definition of gender. Consequently, gender becomes a liquid category. It is solid like ice and liquid like water; and it evaporates like mist. Furthermore, socialization tells us that there exists no absolute identification of gender. From this perspective, there are no right or wrong definitions of gender because gender results from how each society socializes people into gender roles.

For black theology of liberation, whatever type of gender

relationships take place in a community, the key is not the description of the genders but the presence or absence of liberation and the practice of freedom. In other words, socialization states that when babies are born, they can become any gender that society socializes them to be. This suggests a radical possibility because, if the privileges that come along with being male over against women are created by human beings (who go against the spirit of divine liberation), then human beings (who work with the spirit to practice freedom) can bring about social change to remove these privileges from the male gender.

Human societies use various ways to produce a desired gender (that is, the cultural category and dynamic process of socialization). The family remains the basic unit for modeling male and female genders. Other factors of influence are schools, sports, visual and audio entertainment, sex roles, jobs and professions, church and other faith institutions, news media, languages, myths, rituals, laws and race. Especially within the United States of North America, the capitalist system sets the broader context for all definitions and formations of gender. This political economic structure maintains a bottom line culture of profit making at the expense of the majority of the people. The root of the profit culture is private ownership of capital and wealth by a small elite group of families headed by men.

Even more specifically, capitalist democracy in the United States means putting the minority of certain males of a certain race as the primary occupants of power positions and owners of wealth and capital. Immediately, we notice a hierarchy of gender, as well as class and race. This capitalist democracy hierarchy of the minority over the majority thrives on seeing another human being as someone to be used and dominated for profit and the accumulation of more wealth. From the arrival of the first permanent, English speaking European colonies in Jamestown, Virginia (in 1607) to the 1787 U.S. constitutional convention in Philadelphia, Pennsylvania, every foundation of the U.S.A. is based on male superiority. This male gender hierarchy has become so ingrained in both women's and men's hearts and heads that no one even questions the pervasive reality of power positions and wealth ownership belonging to a minority U.S. population – men of a certain racial grouping. From 1607 to the 21st century, voting and laws have not dislodged this entrenched capitalist, democratic minority of men.[5]

In this process of socialization, black men experience a double male gender reality; and both are negative. On the one hand, the larger culture of white society defines black men as subordinate to white men. African American men are socialized as a male gender, but as men who are subordinate to the racial supremacy of another male gender. On the other hand, within the African American community, black men are socialized to adopt the normative definition of the male gender which is established and defined by the larger white male culture. As a result, black men strive towards and enjoy male privileges over black women and children within the African American family and community. When black men adopt and implement the patriarchy of the larger white male culture, they can act out a very sinful and potentially deadly force on those around them. Specifically, too often, African American men store up both their frustrations and anger against white men with power and then release these two demons onto the women, children, and other black men within their own families and communities.[6]

To sum up, the white male culture gives the norm for what it means to be a black man; and therefore African American men pursue this norm. But to imitate this goal outside of the black community and family means accepting one's black manhood as subordinate to white manhood. At the same time, problems with white men with power and wealth outside of the African American context lead black men to see their home or their community as their royal domains where they are king and everyone else serves as their subjects. In a word, black men experience a state of victimization by white male superiority; and they simultaneously enjoy male privileges at home and in their neighborhoods.

Moreover, a system of white male culture in the U.S.A. not only sets the norm for what is a male gender, it creates and perpetuates stereotypes about the black male gender. Thus, black men can never fully reach the norm set by white patriarchy because black men, though males, are not white. At the very same time as they experience this barrier blocking them from realizing the norm, they suffer from a barrage of sinful stereotypes.[7] The visual and audio media in North America image blacks as entertainers through the professions of sports (i.e., Michael Jordan), comedy (i.e., Eddie Murphy), and the military (i.e., Colin Powell). Black men, in the broader culture, are portrayed as being more physical, powerful, and stronger, meaning more sensuous and sexy. As the perfect sexual supermen, African American males are seen as connoisseurs of the sexual act, having the most endurance and physical equipment, and possessing a being (i.e., an ontology) motivated by a life in pursuit of the sexual act. Black men, in the logic of these myths, are more emotional, volatile and unpredictable. Likewise, they lack intelligence and the values of reason, thoughtfulness, academic insight, and deliberate judgement. This false picture goes on to say that African American males are untrustworthy in the areas of wealth and finance, while they have a natural gift of being criminals and engaging in illegal activity. They do not like to work or work hard and are irresponsible. For instance, they are not leaders, but followers. Furthermore, in these stereotypes, they also abandon their children and depend on black women or on white people to back them up.

African American men can do one of the two things. They can accept this understanding of the black male gender or they can choose to create something new. If they accept the white male culture and practices of male gender and the stereotypes that go along with them, then African American males should honestly admit that they suffer as victims of a larger structure, but, at the same time, black men are also making conscious choices to carry out the negative aspects of this structure. If this sinful choice is made, it has devastating consequences on black women and children in particular. Basically, one opts for very harmful power and control strategy and tactics against African American women. This takes place in the following ways: persuading black women that they should support the black man at all costs because he is a victim of white male oppression; intimidation, emotional abuse, and isolation of black women; denying and or minimizing any wrong doing but blaming the women; using children against women; using male privilege (such as, acting like the king of the castle or making all final decisions); and carrying out economic abuse, verbal threats, physical violence, or sexual violence (i.e., through direct physical force or nagging pursuit).

Refusing to opt for this negative and abusive choice, African American men can start to reconstruct what it means to be a new heterosexual male. We begin first with accepting the love of God which is in all black men. At the root, all harmful attitudes and actions against black women and children flow from black men's lack of self love. But self love can only come to reality when men understand and feel a love which is greater than any one person. It is a transcendent love, a divine love, a love which comes from the collective body. In this sense, it is not an individual love, but a love which floods the very being of the individual as a gift from love proceeding from the group level into the soul of the individual. Divine love found within black men corresponds to a sacred love for and from the family and community. Ultimate love or God's love means that God loves black men in spite of the broken vessels that they are.

Such a love has profound implications for the ongoing struggle for the African American community to achieve an inclusive and holistic liberation and to practice freedom. The movement for liberation cannot be sustained through the inevitable ups and downs and forward and backward steps, and the high successes as well as the stinging defeats unless black men love themselves. And the starting point is recognition and acceptance of God's unconditional love. Indeed, God's love grants the black man a power which gives his allegiance not to any earthly demonic structures or individual authority figures, but to something which transcends the boundaries of this world. Equipped with this love and power in one's feelings and one's intellect, in one's heart and one's head, African American men no longer will have to choose the negative and abusive options.

On the contrary, the struggle for liberation and the practice of freedom become one's vocation from God. This vocation places all social relations, uncontrolled cravings, negative pulls of the black male ego, endless tasks, and incorrect focus on the individual self into perspective. Thus, self-love is not a self-centered practice or feeling where one's worldview and lifestyle become "I think therefore I am" or "I pursue money, profit and wealth, therefore I am." Nor does this love indicate a touchy-feely state of being in the world. It is love of self founded on divine love which subordinates the lifestyle of the individual African American male for the liberation and practice of freedom of the family, community and all humankind.

A spirituality of love from God acts as the foundation for the definition of the self. Spirituality, however, manifests in the material, real, tangible world. A true heterosexual black male, full of God's love, takes a stand against a host of domestic desires and deeds. He speaks out against various discriminations as it pertains to race, gender, class, sexual orientation, and ecological issues. The starting point and yardstick remain justice and freedom for all, beginning with the least in society and the poor. When he lives in the world with this type of talk and walk, he inevitably meets those who wish to maintain their privileges of race, class, gender, sexual orientation, and human cravings over all of God's creation. Therefore, when an African American man stands with the majority (i.e., the poor and the least in society) in contrast to the minority (i.e., capitalist democracy for the few who own wealth and power), his very reason for living will be challenged. Those with power will use different ways to challenge the very notion of God's love for black men and, consequently, black men's divine given self-love. But the more African American men withstand this trial and the more they feel good about themselves, the more likely there will be a healthy black family and community. Again, good feelings and healthy conditions result from engagement in struggle for intentional self-transformation and collective transformation. Transformation requires work; work requires discipline; discipline requires sacrifice; sacrifice requires motivation from a higher calling; a calling requires a recognition of being loved; being loved empowers one to love oneself and thereby free others from the external structures and internal demons in their lives.

For Christians, Jesus stands for this liberation love. God's work in and through Jesus did not depend on and had nothing to do with the fact that Jesus was a man biologically. However, the way Jesus constructed his male gender gives us a model for the construction of today's new black heterosexual, male. Because he was so caught up in the mission of the spirit who had anointed him to be with the poor on the divine-human journey to practice freedom, Jesus loved himself enough based on this spiritual vocation. The most striking example shows in how Jesus talked to, spent time with, listened to, answered the questions of, healed, and empowered women to become their full selves. He accepted both male and female disciples. He commissioned women, as well as men, to carry out the work of justice from God. Women became the first preachers to proclaim the liberation revelation of Jesus as the risen Christ. Jesus ordained them to carry forth the good news that death caused by a political crucifixion no longer had the final word. In fact, he broke the status quo boundaries around and oppressive definitions of what it meant to be both male and female.

Any black male who believes and acts as if any black female is secondary, represents the work of the Anti-Christ. He goes against the entire birth, life, ministry, and legacy of Jesus the Anointed One. For the followers of Christianity, he has stepped intentionally or unintentionally away from the path of life, but onto the walk way to destroy the African American community.

A theological reconstruction of the black male consists of not only the love of God and the life of Jesus, but also realizes that God is black for African American males in the United States. To be made in the image of God compels black males to make a leap into the blackness of God's essence for them. To worship and surrender total allegiance to something or somebody alien to African American males is slow self-destruction and internal spiritual death. A black God affirms every physical characteristic of what the U.S.A. calls black. And God says it is good. This brings about a subversive move precisely because a spiritual vision, value, and vocation overcomes all the negative stereotypes forced upon and propagated against black males. God as spirit manifests in the phenotype (i.e., the biological and physical characteristics) of African American males. Such a claim can cause a disruption in the minds of men.

Specifically, for too long, black males have been on their knees praying to an old white man with grey hair. On the theological level, this is nonsense since black folk represent the image of God. Therefore, theologically, God by necessity is black if black folk are images of God. And on the psychological and emotional level, praying to a white male god has meant, in the context of North America, black people willingly giving their complete selves to the very same image of the system and structure of the supremacy of whites over blacks. This old, grey haired, white god has been one of the deepest causes for black self-hatred. In this sinful faith of self-hatred, black men can only be themselves by first becoming white. However, whites nor blacks are divine in and of themselves. God is black for African American males due to the divine choosing of those on the bottom of society's scale. Again, God's spirit is a spirit of liberation and she chooses to manifest herself as black to be with the "little ones" of this earth. When African American men go against their black culture, context and characteristics, they oppose God for their own human liberation.

Not only is God black, God is both father God and mother God. First of all, the being of God is a spirit. Human speech simply gives various verbal symbols for this divine spirit of liberation and freedom.[8] For example, Jesus (i.e., the spirit's decisive revelation for Christians) has various human symbols for divine power – the Savior, the Liberator, Son of God, Son of Man, Mary's Baby, Lilly of the Valley, the Shepherd, the Alpha and the Omega, etc. Again, human beings receive the spirit and attempt to name the revelation in the best manner possible to paint the presence and power of God. The spirit cannot be contained within one human symbol. Specifically, the human symbol or description called "father God" represents only one alternative. We cannot limit the power and presence of God to one gender. God gave birth to all of humanity and all of creation. God watched over this creation and nurtured it, protected it, taught it, and gave/gives life to it. Therefore, God's spirit also assumes or takes on the human symbol or gender of "mother God." God is both mother God and father God. The male symbol for God (i.e., father God) represents only one gender and, left by itself, excludes over seventy per cent of the African American church and over fifty percent of the black community.[9]

Theologically we all are made in God's image. Therefore, black women reflect the female gender of God – mother God. When black men continue to pray to father God only, they are perpetuating and protecting African American men's privileges and expectations of automatic entitlement. Similarly, they continue to subordinate black women and discount the divine reality in their ebony sisters. Men, and unfortunately with the help of some women, have established gender hierarchy with a patriarchal God who says he has all power. But this power is limited to one gender. Likewise this power is limited to hierarchy and not equality. A limited divinity is not God, but the creation of black men who benefit from assuming that African American women are secondary creations of God. A further example of this claim is seen with the clear contrast in the emphasis on blackness or Africanness on the part of black men. Why is it that black men do not fight as hard for the female gender of God as they struggle for the black and African dimensions of God?

An African connection does occupy a prominent position in the reconstruction of the new black male. African Americans have a mixed background and identity. Centuries have made them integral to what has become the space and time called the United States of North America. Simultaneously, however, a black man recognizes and develops the legacy of his African ancestry. The African part of the black male is the very difference which distinguishes his divine identity. In the belief structures of West African peoples (i.e., the ancestors of the majority of present day black Americans), sacred and secular operate together. Otherwise, God would be impotent and missing from some aspect of God's reality. If black men are men, then they respond to a calling which covers all aspects of everyday life in the U.S.A. Faith stretches beyond a ritual on Sunday or a private prayer. The presence of faith translates into the struggle of liberation and the practice of freedom in the private, public, personal and political spheres of breathing. The God of liberation instructs the new black male to be a man wherever he breathes.

Furthermore, the West African legacy gives a black man a sense of respect based on how well he participates with, takes care of, and shares in the African American family. It cuts against the notion of the absent, authoritative, non-vulnerable, domineering North American male who expects entitlement simply because of his biological make up and a negative affirmative action based simply on his male gender. The West African influence, moreover, centers a black man on the well being of the community. "I am because we are" and "without community, one is an animal" become the hallmark of the African American male's lifestyle. The new black male opposes capitalist individualism of me-first and profit-first at the expense of the collective. Such a deadly practice and demonic religion positions one race or gender or class or sexual orientation "first" above others. Therefore, black men in North America grow out of a world view and way of life handed down from West Africa.

Planting Seeds

I am part of two groups attempting to talk through and walk into what it means to be a new heterosexual black male. The first example consists of black Christian, heterosexual males, most of whom are married to or in relationships with African American women; and we are all members of black churches.[10] This first instance is what we call a men's cell group. Meeting twice a month, on Saturdays at 7 a.m., the cell group has at least 14 members. This space and time expresses a sacred, holistic perspective on life. We engage in prayer and Bible study, as well as read various types of liberation materials from a host of disciplines and subject matters. We have read black theology and womanist theology materials; we have spent time covering literature on the plight and prospects for the black male in America. We have learned about meditation and spiritual formation. We also look at documentary videos from Rev. Adam Clayton Powell, Jr., Martin Luther King, Jr., Paul Robeson, to John Coltrane, Fred Hampton, various black preachers and black churches, and more.

The sharing on political, cultural, economic, local, national, and international events provides, in addition, a location for individual reflection on the joys (i.e., praise reports) and pains (i.e., prayer concerns) of each individual black man in the room. Tears have been shed as well as discussions about working with poor black folk and protesting some injustices in the African American community. An ongoing focus is how to become strong black Christian males who can accept the love of God and love of the self and work with the black woman to enhance the African American family and community. However, the ultimate goal is to participate in the well being of the least in every society of the world. Some of the men involve themselves in areas of direct political work, economic development or grooming a new generation of young black men through rites of passage programs. We have engaged in heated debates on black parenting and on the ups and downs of Wall Street. Self-criticism has become a part of the group, especially when we discuss how we participate in the liberation of poor blacks; this manifests in the areas of providing jobs, enhancing black health, writing on behalf of the least, proclaiming the gospel of good news and justice for the oppressed, and creating right relationships in other ongoing projects.

The second process of reconstructing black maleness takes place in a black theology and womanist theology course which I teach with my wife Linda E. Thomas, a womanist anthropologist and theologian.[11] Since 1997, we have been co-teaching this course every spring, both at her graduate school and at mine. To our knowledge, this remains the first and only such course co-taught by a black theologian and a womanist theologian. In terms of the syllabi, lectures, and the co-managing of the classes, we have tried to model what black female-black male and black theology and womanist theology relationships mean as practical intellectual disciplines of equality and freedom. Usually, during a ten week quarter, we spend two weeks on each of five social science categories – race, gender, class, sexual orientation, and the ecology.

For instance, when we begin with race, the first week offers the black theologian's perspective on the thought and life of race. Students read theological interpretations of race. During class, I, as the black theologian, present a lecture which includes both a social science definition of race and a theological interpretation of race.

Both theoretical and personal experiences are brought to bear in this teaching method. Then my wife, the womanist anthropologist and theologian, responds from a womanist perspective. Next we both engage in a dialogue, and sometimes, a debate. Students enter the conversation after this moment. The next week, we continue on race; but the womanist lecture is presented. After the lecture, the black theologian responds; conversation and debate unfold between the two professors, and then students join in. The presupposition is that throughout this conversational format of theory, personal experience, and seeking individual and collective transformation, we seek to clarify and create what it means to be new black men and women. From that particularity, other participants bring their full intellect and personal experiences into the discussion.

In addition to theoretical constructs and personal stories, what I am learning is that it is one thing to write and teach about the creation of a new African American male gender. It is another to co-teach a course with a womanist and the womanist is my wife. More specifically, I mean that the course does not end in the class room. We continue the discussion in our daily living, either verbally or in practice. Since we both are tenured professors, authors, teachers, lecturers, international travelers, and co-parents, there really is no credible, compelling or consistent theological excuse for assuming that the "man" has to do such and such because he is a "man." Therefore, when we discuss the five categories from our class room teachings, we resume this dialogue on the other side of the threshold of the academic space. In fact, in a very real sense, the title of this course could be "Black Theology and Womanist Theology: from the kitchen to the classroom." Indeed, the black male has to learn a gender which opens itself to challenges and transformation in all areas of what it means to be loved by a God who wants liberation for the poor. Some of these inclusive dimensions and holistic areas are vulnerability, protection, intimacy, political protest, self-critique, new forms of leadership both in the home, church, and broader civic society, and other frontiers. This essay is a result of the creative intellectual challenges posed to me by my wife, a womanist scholar who draws her suggestions, wisdom, and criticisms from the areas of theology and anthropology and from her life experiences.

The question of the creation of a new heterosexual black male gender, from the perspective of black theology, flows like a weaving process. It never progresses in a straight line. Like all scientific discoveries, quality relationships, and the implementation of the finest visions, becoming something new unleashes a quilting and layering process. Sometimes, the newness reveals itself as bright as the morning sun or as clear as the brilliance of a black summer night. Other times the struggle falters and goes backwards, gripped in the old hand of male privilege. But what has to be the foundation of this crucial effort is an openness to what black theology claims so adamantly. That is to say, God loves the poor and those who work on justice for the least in society. Here marks the purpose for the revelation of Jesus the anointed one on earth. Male chauvinism (i.e., the attitude of superiority), male privileges (i.e., the practice of this attitude), and patriarchy (i.e., the system which exists in spite of how nice individual men are) cut against everything that God, Jesus, and West African ancestors have called black men to be, say, and do. The good news is that African American men will be fully human when black women achieve their full humanity. I am because we are. And we are part of a faith and a tradition that says, "God may not come when you call God, but God is always right on time."

Notes

1. See Dwight N. Hopkins, "Black Women's Spirituality of Funk," chapter 2, in his *Shoes That Fit Our Feet* (Maryknoll, N.Y.: Orbis Books, 1993); Garth Baker-Fletcher, "New Males? Same Ole Same Ole," and "Taking Sisters Seriously," chapters 2 and 3, in his *Xodus: An African American Male Journey* (Minneapolis,

MN: Fortress Press, 1996); James H. Cone, "Black Theology, Black Churches and Black Women, chapter 6, in his *For My People: Black Theology and The Black Church, Where Have We Been and Where Are We Going?* (Maryknoll, N.Y.: Orbis Books, 1984); and James H. Evans, "Black Theology and Black Feminism," *Journal of Religious Thought*, 38/1 Spring-Summer, 1981.

2. Since I'm mainly concerned with black heterosexual males in this essay, please refer to the following essays by Horace Griffin, a self-identified, African American gay, Christian: "Their Own Received Them Not: African American Lesbians and Gays in Black Churches," *Journal of Theology and Sexuality*, (Spring, 2000); "Revisioning Christian Ethical Discourse on Homosexuality: A Challenge for the 21st Century," *Journal of Pastoral Care* (Summer, 1999); "Giving New Birth: Lesbians, Gays and the 'Family': A Pastoral Care Perspective," *Journal of Pastoral Theology*, (Summer 1993); All see Bill Smith's (a self-identified, African American Gay, Christian) "Liberation As Risky Business," in *Changing Conversations: Religious Reflections & Cultural Analysis*, eds. Dwight N. Hopkins and Sheila Greeve Daveney (New York: Routledge, 1996).

3. See Roger N. Lancaster & Micaela di Leonardo, eds. *The Gender Sexuality Reader* (New York: Routledge, 1997); Steve Pile and Nigel Thrift, eds. *Mapping the Subject: geographies of cultural transformation* (New York: Routledge, 1995); Kwame Anthony Appiah and Henry Louis Gates, Jr., eds. (Chicago: The University of Chicago Press, 1995); Anne McClintock, *Imperial Leather: race, gender and sexuality in the colonial contest* (New York: Routledge, 1995); Colette Guillaumin, *Racism, Sexism, Power and Ideology* (New York: Routledge, 1995); Ruth Frankenberg, *The Social Construction of White Women, Race Matters* (Minneapolis, MN.: The University of Minnesota Press, 1993); Sherry B. Ortner, *Making Gender: The politics and erotics of culture* (Boston, MA.: Beacon Press, 1996); Harry Stecopoulos and Michael Uebel, eds, *Race and the Subject of Masculinities* (Durham, N.C.: Duke University Press, 1997); and Robert J.C. Young, *Colonial Desire: hybridity in theory, culture and race* (New York: Routledge, 1995).

4. I am not referring to the turn to the self of modernity which arose with the Enlightenment in Europe. Indeed, I am arguing in radical contrast to this idea of the self. See Peter Gay, *The Enlightenment: an interpretation* (New York: Vintage, 1968); Antony Flew, *An Introduction to Western Philosophy: ideas and argument from Plato to Popper, revised edition* (New York: Thames and Hudson, 1989); Jonathan Barned, *The Presocratic Philosophers* (New York: Routledge, 1993); David J. Chalmers, *The Conscious Mind: in search of a fundamental theory* (New York: Oxford University Press, 1996); and Simon Critchley and William R. Schroeder, eds. *A Companion to Continental Philosophy* (Malden, Mass: Blackwell Publishers, 1999). For my purposes as it pertains to the lifestyle of the self, here I am particularly drawing on African understandings of culture as "I am because we

are" and "Without community, a person is an animal." See Emmanuel Chukwudi Eze, ed. *Postcolonial African Philosophy: a critical reader* (Malden, Mass: Blackwell Publishers, 1997): Emmanuel Chukwudi Eze, ed. *African Philosophy: an anthology* (Malden, Mass: Blackwell Publishers, 1998); Tsenay Serequeberhan, ed. *African Philosophy: the essential readings* (New York: Paragon House, 1991); P.H. Coetzee and A.P.J. Roux, eds. *The African Philosophy Reader* (New York: Routledge, 1998); and Jacob K. Olupona, ed. *African Traditional Religions in Contemporary Society* (New York: Paragon House, 1991).

5. See Melvin L. Oliver and Thomas M. Shapiro, *Black Wealth/White Wealth: A New Perspective on Racial Inequality* (New York: Routledge, 1995); Marcellus Andrews, *The Political Economy of Hope and Fear: Capitalism and the Black Condition in America* (New York: New York University Press, 1999); Dalton Conley, *Being Black, Living in the Red: race, wealth, and social policy in America* (Berkeley, CA: University of California, 1999); and Nelson W. Aldrich, *Old Money the mythology of America's upper class* (New York: A.A. Knopf, 1988).

6. Examine William H. Grier and Price M. Cobbs, Black Rage (New York: Basic Books, 1968); Ronn Elmore, *How to Love a Black Woman* (New York: Warner Books, 1998); Philip Brian Harper, *Are We Not Men?: masculine anxiety and the problem of African-American identity* (New York: Oxford University Press, 1996); Marcelus Blount & George P. Cunningham, eds., *Representing Black Men* (New York: Routledge, 1996); Iyanla Vanzant, *The Spirit of a Man: a vision of transformation for black men and the women who love them* (New York: Harper Collins Publishers, 1996); Beth E. Richie, *Compelled to Crime: the gender entrapment of battered black women* (New York: Routledge, 1996); Richard Majors and Janet Mancini Billson, *Cool Pose: the dilemmas of black manhood in America* (New York: A Touchstone Book, 1992); and Ernest H. Johnson, *Brothers On The Mend: understanding and healing anger of African-American Men and Women* (New York: Pocket Books, 1998).

7. Review Annie Barner, *Say It Loud: middle-class blacks talk about racism and what to do about it* (Cleveland, Ohio: The Pilgrim Press, 2000); Michael C. Pounds, *Race in Space* (Lanham, MD: The Scarecrow Press, 1999); Patricia Turner, *Ceramic Uncles & Celluloid Mammies: black images and their influence in culture* (New York: Anchor Books, 1994); Leonard Cassuto, *The Inhuman Race: the racial grotesque in American literature and culture* (New York: Columbia University Press, 1997); Lee D. Baker, *From Savage to Negro; anthropology and the construction of race, 1896-1954* (Berkeley: University of California Press, 1998); Thomas F. Gossett, *Race: the history of an idea in America* (New York: Schocken Books, 1971); Mary Pattillo-McCoy, *Black Picket Fences, Privileges and Peril among the Black Middle Class* (Chicago, IL: University of Chicago Press, 1999); and *Without Sanctuary: Lynching Photography in America* (Santa Fe, N.M.: Twin PalmsPublishers, 2000).

8. On the symbolic portrayals of God, see James H. Cone, *A Black Theology of Liberation: twentieth anniversary edition* (Maryknoll, N.Y.: Orbis Books, 1990); and James H. Cone, *God of the Oppressed* (Maryknoll, N.Y.: Orbis Books, 1997).

9. Review the following on the gender dimensions of God, Rosemary Radford Reuther, *Sexism and God-Talk: toward a feminist theology*, (Boston, Mass: Beacon Press, 1993); Kelly Brown Douglas, *The Black Christ* (Maryknoll, N.Y.: Orbis Books, 1994); and Jacquelyn Grant, "Womanist Theology: Black Women's Experience as a Source for Doing Theology, with Special Reference to Christology," *Journal of the Interdenominational Theological Centre*, vol. 13, no. 2, (Spring 1986), reprinted in James H. Cone and Gayraud S. Wilmore, eds. *Black Theology, a documentary history, volume two: 1980-1992* (Maryknoll, N.Y.: Orbis Books, 1993).

10. The majority of the group members belong to Trinity United Church of Christ in Chicago, Illinois. The senior pastor of Trinity, Jeremiah A. Wright, Jr., initiated the idea of black Christian men's cell groups.

11. We are also publishing and continue to do joint writing projects. For instance, see Dwight N. Hopkins and Linda E. Thomas, "Voices from the Margins in the United States," in *The Twentieth Century: A Theological Overview* (Maryknoll, N.Y.: Orbis Books, 1999), ed. Gregory Baum; and Hopkins and Thomas, "Black Theology USA Revisited," in *Journal of Theology for Southern Africa*, March 1998, (University of Cape Town, Cape Town, South Africa).

The Gendered Forms of Racism: A Native American Woman's Perspective

Andrea Smith

A young North American Indian woman was once gang raped by prominent members of an urban Indian community I lived in. When she sought justice, the response of the community was to blame her – she was dividing the community by airing its "dirty laundry." At the same time, however, she had difficulty accessing the mainstream anti-sexual/domestic violence movement. In fact, the year before I began working in sexual assault services in this city, only one Native woman had received services at a rape crisis centre.

This woman's story exemplifies the difficulties women of color face when they are victimized by sexual or domestic violence. In addition, it speaks to the inadequate interpretations that dominates both male-dominated analysis of racism and colonialism and white-dominated analysis of sexism. Communities of color often advocate that women keep silent about sexual and domestic violence in order to maintain a united front against racism. Consequently, women of color are often forced out of their communities in order to access services from domestic violence shelters and rape crisis centres. Unfortunately, racial justice organizing has generally focused on racism as it primarily affects men and has often ignored the gendered forms of racism that women of color face.

Meanwhile, when survivors seek help from white-dominated agencies, they are often told to disassociate themselves from their communities where their abusers are. The underlying philosophy of the white-dominated anti-rape movement is implicit in feminist theorist Susan Brownmiller's statement: [Rape] is nothing more or less than a conscious process of intimidation by which all men keep all women in a state of fear.[1] The notion that rape is "nothing more or less" than a tool of patriarchal control fails to consider how rape also serves as a tool of racism and colonialism. Unfortunately, feminist organizing has generally focused on sexism as it primarily affects white women and has often ignored the racialized and colonial forms of sexism that women of color and Third World women face. This paper explores sexual violence in Native communities as a way to challenge these limiting forms of analysis about gender/race/colonialism that continue to marginalize the experiences of indigenous women, women of color, and women in the Third World.

According to the Mending The Hoop Technical Assistance Project in Minnesota, tribally-based sexual assault advocates believe that a major difficulty in developing comprehensive programs to address sexual assault in tribal communities, particularly sexual violence against adult women, is that many community members believe that sexual violence is "traditional." Historical evidence suggests, however, that sexual violence was rare in Native communities prior to colonization, and that it has served as a primary weapon in the U.S. war against Native nations ever since. Not only have tribal communities adopted European practices of sexual violence, they have largely lost sight of the fact that sexual violence is, in fact, not an Indian tradition. Both these responses reveal a lack of understanding of how sexual violence itself is an act of colonialism and genocide. Far from being traditional, sexual violence is an attack on Native sovereignty itself. As one leader stated at a conference I attended, "as long as we destroy ourselves from the inside, we don't have to worry about anyone on the outside."

Critical racist theorist Kimberle Crenshaw has critiqued the white-dominated anti-violence movement for its lack of attention to racism and classism. Crenshaw analyzes how male-dominated conceptions of race and white-dominated conceptions of gender stand in the way of a clear understanding of violence against women of color. It is inadequate, she argues, to investigate the oppression of women of color by examining race and gender oppressions separately and then putting the two analyses together, because the overlap of racism and sexism transforms the dynamics of both. Instead, Crenshaw advocates replacing the "additive" approach with an "intersectional" perspective that accounts for the overlap. "The problem is not simply that both discourses fail women of color by not acknowledging the 'additional' issue of race or of patriarchy but, rather, that the discourses are often inadequate even to the discrete tasks of articulating the full dimensions of racism and sexism."[2]

Despite her intersectional approach, however, Crenshaw falls short of describing how a politics of intersectionality might fundamentally shift how we analyze sexual/domestic violence. If sexual violence is not simply a tool of patriarchy, but is also a tool of colonialism and racism, then entire communities of color and Third World communities are the victims of sexual violence. As Neferti Tadiar argues, colonial relationships are themselves gendered and sexualized. "[T]he economies and political relations of nations are libindally configured, that is, they are grasped and effected in terms of sexuality. This global and regional fantasy is not, however, only metaphorical, but real insofar as it grasps a system of political and economic practices already at work among these nations.[3] Within this context, according to Tadiar, "the question to be asked...is, "Who is getting off on this? Who is getting screwed and by whom?"[4] Haunani Kay Trask draws similar analysis about US-Hawaii relationships, which she frames in terms of "cultural prostitution."

> "Prostitution" in this context refers to the entire institution which defines a woman (and by extension the "female") as an object of degraded and victimized sexual value for use and exchange through the medium of money. . . . My purpose is not to exact detail or fashion a model but to convey the utter degradation of our culture and our people under corporate tourism by employing "prostitution" as an analytical category. . . .
>
> The point, of course, is that everything in Hawaii can be yours, that is, you the tourist, the non-native, the visitor. The place, the people, the culture, even our identity as a "Native" people is for sale. Thus, Hawaii, like a lovely woman, is there for the taking.[5]

Within the context of colonization of Native nations, sexual violence does not affect Indian men and women in the same way. However, when a Native woman suffers abuse, this abuse is not just attack on her identity as a woman, but on her identity as Native. The issues of colonial, race, and gender oppression cannot be separated. This explains why in my experience as a rape crisis counsellor, every Native survivor I ever counselled said to me at one point, "I wish I was no longer Indian." Women of color do not just face quantitatively more issues when they suffer violence (i.e., less media attention, language barriers, lack of support in the judicial system, etc.) but their experience is qualitatively different from that of white women.

Ann Stoler argues that racism, far from being a reaction to crisis in which racial others are scapegoated for social ills, is a permanent part of the social fabric. "[R]acism is not an effect but a tactic in the internal fission of society into binary opposition, a means of creating 'biologized' internal enemies, against whom society must defend itself."[6] She notes that in the modern state, it is through the constant purification and elimination of racialized enemies within the state that ensures the growth of the national body. "Racism does not merely arise in moments of crisis, in sporadic cleanings. It is internal to the biopolitical state, woven into the web of the social body, threaded through its fabric."[7]

Similarly, Kate Shanley notes that native peoples are a permanent "present absence" in the U.S. colonial imagination, an "absence" that reinforces at every turn the conviction that Native peoples are indeed vanishing and that the conquest of Native lands is justified. Ella Shoat and Robert Stam describe this absence as "an ambivalently repressive mechanism [which] dispels the anxiety in the face of the Indian, whose very presence is a reminder of the initially precarious grounding of the American nation-state itself. In a temporal paradox, living Indians were indeed to 'play dead,' as it were, in order to perform a narrative of manifest destiny in which their role, ultimately, was to disappear."[8] This "absence" is effected through the metaphorical transformation of Native bodies into a pollution from which the colonial body must purify itself. As white Californians described in 1860s, Native people were "the dirtiest lot of human beings on earth." They wear "filthy rags, with their persons unwashed, hair uncombed and swarming with vermin."[9] The following 1885 Proctor & Gamble ad for Ivory Soap also illustrates this equation between Indian bodies and dirt.

> We were once factious, fierce and wild
> In peaceful arts unreconciled
> Our blankets smeared with grease and stains
> From buffalo meat and settler's veins

>Through summer's dust and heat content
>From moon to moon unwashed we went
>But IVORY SOAP came like a ray
>Of light across our darkened way
>And now we're civil, kind and good
>And keep the laws as people should
>We wear our linen, lawn and lace
>As well as folks with paler face
>And now I take, where'er we go
>This cake of IVORY SOAP to show
>What civilized my squaw and me
>And made us clean and fair to see.[10]

In the colonial imagination, Native bodies are also immanently polluted with sexual sin. Albert Cave, Robert Warrior, H.C. Porter, and others have demonstrated that Christian colonizers often linked Native peoples to the biblical Canaanites, both worthy of mass destruction.[11] What makes Canaanites supposedly worthy of destruction in the biblical narrative and Indian peoples supposedly worthy of destruction in the eyes of their colonizers is that they both personify sexual sin. In the Bible, Canaanites commit acts of sexual perversion in Sodom (Gen. 19:1-29), are the descendents of the unsavory relations between Lot and his daughters (Gen. 19:30-38), are the descendents of the sexually perverse Ham (Gen. 9:22-27), and prostitute themselves in the service of their gods (Gen. 28:21-22; Deut. 28:18; 1 Kings 14:24; 2 Kings 23:7; Hosea 4:13; Amos. 2:7).

Similarly, Native peoples, in the eyes of the colonizers, are marked by their sexual perversity. Alexander Whitaker, a minister in Virginia, wrote in 1613: "They live naked in bodie, as if their shame of their sinne deserved to covering: Their names are as naked as their bodie: They esteem it a virtue to lie, deceive, and steale as their master the divell teacheth them."[12] Furthermore, according to Bernadino de Minaya: "Their [the Indians'] marriages are not a sacrament but a sacrilege. They are idolatrous, libidinous, and commit sodomy. Their chief desire is to eat, drink, worship heathen idols, and commit bestial obscenities."[13]

Because Indian bodies are "dirty," they are considered sexually violable and "rapable." That is, in patriarchal thinking, only a body that is "pure" can be violated. The rape of bodies that are considered inherently impure or dirty simply does not count. For instance, prostitutes have almost an impossible time being believed if they are raped because the dominant society considers the prostitute's body undeserving of integrity and violable at all times. Similarly, the history of mutilation of Indian bodies, both living and dead, makes it clear to Indian people that they are not entitled to bodily integrity, as these examples suggest:

> I saw the body of White Antelope with the privates cut off, and I heard a soldier say he was going to make a tobacco-pouch out of them.[14]

> At night, Dr. Rufus Choate, [and] Lieutenant Wentz C. Miller . . . went up the ravine, decapitated the dead Qua-ha-das, and placing the heads in some gunny sacks, brought them back to be boiled out for future scientific knowledge.[15]

> Each of the braves was shot down and scalped by the wild volunteers, who out with their knives and cutting two parallel gashes down their backs, would strip the skin from the quivering flesh to make razor straps of.[16]

> Dr. Turner, of Lexington, Iowa, visited this solitary grave [of Black Hawk] and robbed it of its tenant . . . and sent the body to Alton, Illinois, where the skeleton was wired together. [It was later returned] but here it remained but a short time ere vandal hands again carried it away and placed it in the Burlington, Iowa Geographical and Historical Society, where it was consumed by fire in 1855.[17]

One more dexterous than the rest, proceeded to flay the chief's [Tecumseh's] body; then, cutting the skin in narrow strips . . . at once, a supply of razor-straps for the more "ferocious" of his brethren.[18]

Andrew Jackson . . . supervised the mutilation of 800 or so Creek Indian corpses – the bodies of men, women and children that he and his men massacred – cutting off their noses to count and preserve a record of the dead, slicing long strips of flesh from the bodies to tan and turn into bridle reins.[19]

A few nights after this, some soldiers dug Mangus' body out again and took his head and boiled it during the night, and prepared the skull to send to the museum in New York.[20]

As Stoler explains, this process of racialized colonization, "[T]he more 'degenerates' and 'abnormals' [in this case Native peoples] are eliminated, the lives of those who speak will be stronger, more vigorous, and improved. The enemies are not political adversaries, but those identified as external and internal threats to the population. Racism is the condition that makes it acceptable to put [certain people] to death in a society of normalization.[21]

Tadiar's description of colonial relationships as an enactment of the "prevailing mode of heterosexual relations" is useful because it underscores the extent to which U.S. colonizers view the subjugation of women of the Native nations as critical to the success of the economic, cultural and political colonization.[22] Stoler notes that the imperial discourses on sexuality "cast white women as the bearers of more racist imperial order."[23] By extension, Native women as bearers of a counter-imperial order pose a supreme threat to the imperial order. Native women continue to be threatening because of their ability to reproduce the next generation of peoples who can resist colonization. While the bodies of both Indian men and women have been marked by sexual violence, Ines Hernandez-Avila notes that the bodies of Native women have been particularly targeted for abuse because of their capacity to give birth. "It is because of a Native American woman's sex that she is hunted down and slaughtered, in fact, singled out, because she has the potential through childbirth to assure the continuance of the people."[24] David Stannard points out that control over women's reproductive abilities and destruction of women and children are essential in destroying a people. If the women of a nation are not disproportionately killed, then that nation's population will not be severely affected. He says that Native women and children were targeted for wholesale killing in order to destroy the Indian nations.[25] This is why colonizers such as Andrew Jackson recommended that troops systematically kill Indian women and children after massacres in order to complete extermination. Symbolic and literal control over their bodies is important in the attack on Native people, as these examples attest:

> When I was in the boat, I captured a beautiful Carib woman . . . I conceived desire to take pleasure . . . I took a rope and thrashed her well, for which she raised such unheard screams that you would not have believed your ears. Finally we came to an agreement in such a manner that I can tell you that she seemed to have been brought up in a school of harlots.[26]

> Two of the best looking of the squaws were lying in such a position, and from the appearance of the genital organs and of their wounds, there can be no doubt that they were first ravished and then shot dead. Nearly all of the dead were mutilated.[27]

> One woman, big with child, rushed into the church, clasping the altar and crying for mercy for herself and unborn babe. She was followed, and fell pierced with a dozen lances . . . the child was torn alive from the yet palpitating body of its mother, first plunged into the holy water to be baptized, and immediately its brains were dashed out against a wall.[28]

> The Christians attacked them with buffets and beatings. . . . Then they behaved with such temerity and shamelessness that

the most powerful rule of the island had to see his own wife raped by a Christian officer.[29]

I heard one man say that he had cut a woman's private parts out, and had them for exhibition on a stick. I heard another man say that he had cut the fingers off of an Indian, to get the rings off his hand. I also heard of numerous instances in which men had cut out the private parts of females, and stretched them over the saddlebows and some of them over their hats.[30]

American Horse said of the massacre at Wounded Knee:

The fact of the killing of the women, and more especially the killing of the young boys and girls who are to go to make up the future strength of the Indian people is the saddest part of the whole affair and we feel it very sorely.[31]

While the era of Indian massacres in their more explicit form in North America has past, this practice of controlling Native women's ability to reproduce continues in new forms. The General Accounting Office released a study in November 1976, indicating that Native women were being sterilized without informed consent. Dr. Connie Uri (Cherokee/Choctaw) conducted further investigations leading her to estimate that 25% of all Native women of childbearing age had been sterilized without their informed consent, with sterilization rates as high as 80% on some reservations.[32] This understanding of Native peoples as dirty and with a sexuality that threatens U.S. security – a view which undergirded the population control movement against Native peoples – was echoed in the comments of one doctor in his attempt to rationalize the mass sterilization of Native women:

People pollute, and too many people crowded too close together cause many of our social and economic problems. These in turn are aggravated by involuntary and irresponsible parenthood.... We also have obligations to the society of which we are part. The welfare mess, as it has been called, cries out for solutions, one of which is fertility control.³³

Herbert Aptheker describes the logical consequences of this sterilization movement:

> The ultimate logic of this is crematoria; people are themselves constituting the pollution and inferior people in particular, then crematoria become really vast sewerage projects. Only so may one understand those who attend the ovens and concocted and conducted the entire enterprise; those "wasted" – to use U.S. army jargon reserved for colonial hostilities – are not really, not fully people.³⁴

While sterilization abuse has curbed somewhat with the institution of informed consent policies, it has reappeared in the form of dangerous contraceptives such as Norplant and Depo-Provera. These are both extremely risky examples of the long-acting hormonal contraceptives that have been pushed on Indian women.³⁵ Depo-Provera, a known carcinogen which has been condemned as an inappropriate form of birth control by several national women's health organizations, was routinely used on Indian women through Indian Health Services (IHS) before it was approved by the FDA in 1992 ("Taking"). It was particularly used for Indian women with disabilities. The reason given – hygenics. Depo-Provera prevents Native women with disabilities from having their periods, thus keeping them "cleaner" for their caretakers. Once again, Native women's bodies are viewed as inherently dirty, in need of cleansing and purification. The Phoenix IHS policy in the 1980s, according to Raymond Jannet, had the following rationale: "We use it to stop their periods. There is nothing else that will do it. To have to change a pad on someone developmentally disabled, you've got major problems. The fact that they become infertile while on it is a side benefit" ("Taking"). Jannet argues that Depo-Provera helps girls with emotions from their periods. "Depo-Provera turned them back into their sweet, poor, handicapped selves. I take some pride in being a pioneer in that regard" ("Taking"). But, he said, while he has no problems using it on Indian women, "I will not be going out and using it on attractive 16-year-old girls who one day hope to become mothers" ("Taking").

The colonization of Native women's bodies continues today. When I served as a non-violent witness for the Chippewa spear fishers in the 1980s who were being harassed by white racist mobs, one white harasser carried as sign saying "Save a fish, spear a pregnant squaw." During the 1990 Mohawk crisis in Oklahoma, a white mob surrounded the ambulance of a native woman who was attempting to leave the Mohawk reservation because she was hemorrhaging after having given birth. She was forced to "spread her legs" to prove she had given birth. The police at the scene refused to intervene. An Indian man was arrested for "wearing a disguise" (he was wearing jeans) and he was brutally beaten, with his testicles crushed. Two women from Chicago WARN (the organization I belong to) went to Oklahoma to videotape this crisis. They were arrested and held in custody for eleven hours without being charged, and were told that they could not go to the bathroom unless a male police officer could watch. The place in which they were held was covered with pornographic magazines.

This colonial desire to subjugate Indian women's bodies was quite apparent when, in 1982, Stuart Kasten marketed a new video, "Custer's Revenge," in which players gets points each time they, in the form of Custer, rape an Indian woman. The slogan of the game is "When you score, you score." He describes the game as "a fun sequence where the woman is enjoying a sexual act willingly." According to the promotional material:

> You are General Custer. Your dander's up, your pistol's wavin'. You've hog-tied a ravishing Indian maiden and have a chance to rewrite history and even up an old score. Now, the Indian maiden's hands may be tied, but she's not about to take it lying down, by George! Help is on the way. If you're to get revenge, you'll have to rise to the challenge, dodge a tribe of flying arrows

and protect your flanks against some downright mean and prickly cactus. But if you can stand pat and last past the strings and arrows — You can stand last. Remember? Revenge is sweet (promotional material).

Many feminist theorists have argued that there is a connection among patriarchy's disregard for nature, for women, and for indigenous peoples. It is the same colonial/patriarchal mind that seeks to control the sexuality of women and indigenous peoples that also seeks to control nature.[36] As Shoat and Stam explain, "Colonized people are projected as body rather than mind, much of the colonized world was seen as raw material rather than as mental activity and manufacture."[37]

Certainly, even today, colonizers justify the theft of Native lands on the grounds that Native peoples did not or do not properly control or subdue nature. For instance, among the Christian Right, John Eidsmoe contends that Christians never stole Indian land. He argues that since Native people did not privatize land, and since their communities had not been "established by God," then Europeans had a right to seize the land from them.[38] And furthermore, while Christianity may have been forced on Native people, "millions of people are in heaven today as a result."[39] As Pat Robertson states:

> These tribes are . . . in an arrested state of social development. They are not less valuable as human beings because of that, but they offer scant wisdom or learning or philosophical vision that can be instructive to a society that can feed the entire population of the earth in a single harvest and send spacecraft to the moon. . . . Except for our crimes, our wars and our frantic pace of life, what we have is superior to the ways of primitive peoples. . . . Which life do you think people would prefer: freedom in an enlightened Christian civilization or the suffering of subsistence living and superstition in a jungle? You choose.[40]

Immanuel Wallerstein argues that "racism is meant to keep people inside the work system [at a state of marginalization], not eject them from it."[41] In the case of Native peoples, however, who have an unemployment rate on reservations of about 80 percent, the intent of racism is to exclude them. Because the majority of the energy resources in this country are on Indian lands, the continued existence of Indian people is a threat to capitalist operations. Thus, the connection between the colonization of Native bodies and Native lands is not simply metaphorical but is rooted in material realities.

In addition, one way in which capitalism has succeeded in continuing its unrelenting assault against the environment is that certain populations become deemed as "surplus" populations and hence either worthy repositories of environment waste or scapegoats of environmental crises in need of population control. Samir Amin describes this process as "apartheid," where "sacrifices imposed on some do not carry the same weight as the benefits obtained by others."[42] Those peoples who have already been rendered dirty, impure, and hence expendable are then forced to face the most immediate consequences of environmental destruction. Unfortunately for colonizers, it is not easy to contain environmental degradation to those populations deemed expendable.

It is not an accident that 100 percent of uranium production takes place on or near Indian land.[43] Nor is it a coincidence that Native reservations are often targeted for toxic waste dumps. To date, over 50 reservations have been target for waste dumps.[44] In addition, military and nuclear testing also takes place almost exclusively on Native lands. For instance, there have already been at least 650 nuclear explosions on Western Shoshone land at the Nevada test site. Fifty percent of these underground tests have leaked radiation into the atmosphere.[45] Native peoples, the expendable ones, are situated to suffer the brunt of environmental destruction so that colonizers can continue to be in denial about the fact that they will also eventually be affected.

A case in point is the current plan to relocate all nuclear wastes into a permanent high-level nuclear waste repository in Yucca Mountain on Shoshone land, for a cost of $3.25 billion. Yucca Mountain is located on an active volcanic zone where kiloton bombs are exploded nearby, thus increasing the risks of radioactive leakage.[46] In addition, if this plan is approved, the proposed repository on Yucca Mountain would receive nuclear wastes throughout the U.S. Only five states would not be affected by the transportation of high-level radioactive wastes. With up to 4,000 shipments of radioactive waste crossing the U.S. annually, trucking industry statistics reveal that up to 50 accidents per year could occur during the 30 year period that nuclear waste would stream to Yucca Mountain.[47]

Katsi Cook, Mohawk midwife, argues that this attack upon nature is yet another attack on Native women's bodies because the effects of toxic and radiation poisoning are most apparent in their effect on women's reproductive systems.[48] In the areas where there is uranium mining, such as in Four Corners and the Black Hills, Indian people face skyrocketing rates of cancer, miscarriages, and birth defects. Children growing up in Four Corners are developing ovarian and testicular cancers at 15 times the national average.[49] Meanwhile, Indian women on Pine Ridge experience a miscarriage rate six times higher than the national average.[50] And on the Akwesasne Mohawk reserve, one of the most polluted areas in the country, the PCBs, DDT, Mirex and HCBs that are dumped into their waters are eventually become stored in women's breast milk.[51] Through the rape of earth, Native women's bodies are raped once again.

As long as Native people continue to live on the lands rich in energy resources that government or corporate interests want, the sexual colonization of Native people will continue. Native bodies will continue to be depicted as expendable and inherently violable as long as they continue to stand in the way of the theft of Native lands. The United States is indeed engaged in a "permanent social war" against the Native bodies, particularly Native women's bodies, which threaten its legitimacy.[52] Colonizers evidently recognize the wisdom of the Cheyenne saying, "A Nation is not conquered until the hearts of the women [and their bodies as well] are on the ground."

Christianity is largely responsible for the introduction of gender violence in Native communities. Missionaries imposed social patterns of gender hierarchy into previously egalitarian Native communities, thus creating the context for abuses of power within these hierarchies. In addition, the large scale introduction of sexual violence in Native communities is largely a result of the Christian boarding school system, which had their beginnings in the 1600s under Jesuit priests along the St. Lawrence River. The system was more formalized in 1870 when the United States Congress set aside funds to erect school facilities to be run by churches and missionary societies.[53] Attendance was mandatory, and children were forcibly taken from their homes for the majority of the year. They were forced to worship Christianity (Native traditions were prohibited), and speak English only.[54] Children were subjected to constant physical and sexual abuse. While not all Native people viewed their boarding school experiences as negative, it appears to be the case that, after the onset of boarding schools in Native communities, abuse becomes endemic within Indian families. Recently, the International Human Rights Association of American Minorities has issued a report which documents the involvement of mainline churches and the federal government in the murder of over 50,000 Native children through the Canadian residential school system. The list of offenses committed by church officials include murder by beating, poisoning, hanging, starvation, strangulation, and medical experimentation. Torture was used to punish children for speaking Aboriginal languages. Children were involuntarily sterilized. In addition, the report found that church clergy, police and business and government officials were involved in maintaining pedophile rings using children from residential schools.[55] The grounds of several schools are also charged with containing unmarked graveyards of children who were murdered, particularly children killed after being born as a result of rapes of Native girls by priests and other church officials in school.[56] While some churches in Canada have taken some minimal steps towards addressing its involvement in this genocidal policy, churches in the United States have not. Furthermore, churches need to do more than apologize for past wrongdoings, they need to provide reparations to Native communities for these wrongdoings and provide concrete, material support for Native struggles today. The fact that the National Council of Churches in the United States has recently tried to lay off its only staff person who works with Native communities suggests, unfortunately, that support for Native communities among churches is lessening rather than improving.

Struggles for sovereignty, racial justice, and liberation from structures of colonialism/neo-colonialism are doomed to failure if they fail to grasp the fact that struggles against sexism are inextricably linked with these struggles. It is through sexism and gender violence that colonialism and racism has been successful. Violence against women is a sovereignty issue. It is time that our organizing efforts reflect this analysis.

Notes

1. Susan Brownmiller, *Against Our Will*. Toronto: Bantam Books, 1986: 5.
2. Kimberle Crenshaw. "The Intersection of Race and Gender," in Kimberle Crenshaw, Neil Gotanda, Gary Peller, and Kendall Thomas (eds) *Critical Race Theory*. New York: New Press, 1996: 360.
3. Neferti Tadiar, "Sexual Economies in the Asia-Pacific Community," publication unknown: 183.
4. Ibid.
5. Haunani Kay Trask. *From a Native Daughter: Colonialism and Sovereignty in Hawai'i*. Monroe: Common Courage Press, 1993: 194.
6. Ann Stoler. *Race and the Education of Desire*. Chapel Hill: Duke University Press, 1997: 59.

7. Ibid.
8. Ella Shoat and Robert Stam. *Unthinking Eurocentricism*. London: Routledge, 1994: 118-119.
9. James Rawis. *Indians of California: The Changing Image*. Norman: University of Oklahoma Press, 1997: 195.
10. Andre Lopez. *Pagans in Our Midst*. Mohawk Nation: Awkwesasne Notes. n.d.: 119. It should be noted, as Paula Allen points out, that native people in fact bathed much more frequently than did Europeans. See Allen, *The Sacred Hoop*. Boston: Beacon Press, 1986: 217.
11. Albert Cave. "Cananites in a Promised Land," *American Indian Quarterly*. Fall 1988: 277-297; H.C. Porter. *The Inconstant Savage*. London: Gerald Duckworth & Co., 1979; Djelai Kadir. *Columbus and the Ends of the Earth*. Berkeley: University of California Press, 1992; Robert Warrior. "Canaanites, Cowboys and Indians," *Anthology of HONOR*, pp. 21-26 (formerly in *Christianity and Crisis*, September 11, 1989).
12. Robert Berkhofer, *The White Man's Indian*. New York: Vintage, 1978: 19.
13. David Stannard, *American Holocaust*, Oxford: Oxford University Press, 1992: 211.
14. In David Wrone and Russel Nelson (eds). *Who's the Savage?* Malabar: Robert Krieger Publishing, 1982: 113.
15. Ibid: 124.
16. Ibid: 90.
17. Ibid: 91.
18. Ibid: 82.
19. Stannard: 121.
20. Wrone: 106.
21. Stoler: 85.
22. Tadiar: 186.
23. Stoler: 35.
24. Ines Hernandez-Avila, "In Praise of Insubordination, or What Makes a Good Woman Go Bad?" in Emilie Buchwald, Pamela R. Fletcher, and Martha Roth (eds). *Transforming a Rape Culture*. Minneapolis: Milkweed, 1993: 386.
25. Stannard: 121.
26. Kirpatrick Sale. *The Conquest of Paradise*. New York: Plume, 1990: 140.
27. Wrone: 123.
28. Wrone: 91.
29. Bartolome Las Casas. *The Devastation of the Indies*, transl. by Herma Briffault. Baltimore: John Hopkins University Press, 1992: 33.
30. The *Sand Creek Massacre: A Documentary History*, New York: Sol Lewis, 1973: 129-130.
31. Stannard: 127.
32. Gayle Mark Jarvis. "The Theft of Life," *WARN Report* n.d.: 13-16. Brint Dillingham. "Indian Women and IHS Sterilization Practices," *American Indian Journal*, January 1977: 27-28; Brint Dillingham. "Sterilization of Native Americans," *American Indian Journal* July

1977: 16-19; "Oklahoma: Sterilization of Native Women Charged to I.H.S." *Akwesasne Notes*, Mid Winter 1989.
33. "Oklahoma:"1 1.
34. Herbert Aptheker, *Racism, Imperialism and Peace*. Minneapolis, MEP Publications: 144.
35. For a more in-depth discussion of the hazards of Depo-Provera and Norplant, see Andrea Smith, "Better Dead Than Pregnant," in Anannya Bhattacharjee and Jael Silliman (eds) *Sex and Surveillance*. Boston: South End Press, forthcoming.
36. Carolyn Merchant. *Death of Nature*. San Francisco: Harper & Row, 1980; Jane Caputi, *Gossips, Gorgons and Crones*. Santa Fe: Bear Publishing, 1993; Rosemary Radford Ruether, *New Woman, New Earth*. Minneapolis: Seabury Press, 1975.
37. Shoat and Stam:138.
38. John Eidsmoe *Columbus and Cortez, Conquerors for Christ*. Green Forest, Arkansas: 1992: 133.
39. Eidsmoe: 140.
40. Pat Robertson, *The Turning Tide*. Dallas: Word Books, 1993: 153.
41. Immanuel Wallerstein, 'The Ideological Tensions of Capitalism: Universalism versus Racism and Sexism," in Etienne Balibar and Immanuel Wallerstein (eds) *Race, Nation, Class*. London, Verso: 29-36.
42. Samir Amin, *Imperialism and Unequal Development*. New York: Monthly Review Press: 142.
43. Winona La Duke, "A Society Based on Conquest Cannot be Sustained," in Richard Hofricher (ed). *Toxic Struggles*. Philadelphia: New Society Publishers, 1993: 99.
44. Conger Beasely, "Dances with Garbage," *E Magazine*. November/December 1991: 40.
45. Valerie Taliman, "Tribes Speak Out On Toxic Assault," *Lakota Times*. December 18, 1991.
46. Ibid.
47. Ibid.
48. Lecture at Indigenous Women's Network Conference at White Earth Reservation, September 17, 1994.
49. Valerie Taliman "Toxic Waste of Indian Lives," *Covert Action* 17, Spring, 1992: 16-22.
50. Harden, *Black Hills PAHA SAPA Report*. August-September 1980: 15.
51. "Contaminated Milk in Mohawk Women," *Sojourner*, April 1994: 11.
52. Stoler: 69.
53. Jorje Noriega. "American Indian Education in the United States: Indoctrination for Subordination to Colonialism." Pp. 37 1-402 in *State of Native America*, edited by M. Annette Jaimes. Boston: South End Press.
54. Frederick Binder and Davis Reimers (Eds.). 1982. *The Way We Lived*. Lexington: D.C. Health and Company.
55. Alan Hughes, "Disturbing Revelations," *The New Internationalist* January-February, 1999.
56. Suzanne Fournier, "Gatherers Mark School's Grim Litany of Death, *The Province* June 4, 1996.

Latin American Feminist Theology and Gender Theories

Silvia Regina de Lima Silva

In this reflection, we want to share about feminist theological production in Latin America in relation to gender theories. The article is limited to a theoretical reflection, but this reflection is a synthesis and the fruit of the process practiced in everyday life by groups of women, the feminist movement, and teaching experiences in seminaries and universities. These lessons have been shared through articles, books, and, above all, in meetings on Feminist Theology on a national, regional and Latin American level.[1]

The first part of this article, a contribution from Tania Maria Sampaio,[2] is an approach to the theories of gender, specifically with epistemological and methodological contributions. The second part begins with a brief synthesis of Latin American and Caribbean Feminist Theology, and we conclude with some of the more relevant contribution of the gender theories to feminist theology.

1. Gender as a Category for Analysis

The use of gender as a category for analysis is a theoretical possibility that responds to the question of the circulation of power and, therefore, is capable of articulating both the confluence of the relationship among sexes, ethnicities and class that cut across the various sectors of humanity. We can, in this way, affirm that not only in the construction and transmission of theory, not only knowledge but also reality is generically[3] constructed. That is, knowledge and reality are marked by the interests and asymmetric relations that subordinate women as well as other social groups.

Among the current issues that appeal to Theology and the Sciences of Religion to involve themselves in the study of gender is the challenge of uncovering these "mechanisms by which the domination of women is reproduced"[4] or that of other social groups, bringing to the forefront historic processes of resistance to oppression. To consider the circumstances in the world today that are marked by processes of exclusion and inferiorization, means not to become paralyzed in the face of the perspective that power resides exclusively in the dominant sector and, consequently, to affirm that this power is dispersed in social relationships of powers that are in a continual state of change.[5]

It must be understood here that these characteristics of social powers in flux are original to the social constructions and can be deconstructed or reconstructed based on other criteria. This paper, then, seeks to question, from the perspective of Theology and the Religious Sciences, the normative processes in the creation of knowledge, academic vocabulary, the selection of contents, and administrative-academic organization. Moreover, in this interrogation, the goal is to denaturalize processes that are socially constructed and to offer an analysis of social power relations.

An analytic procedure that works with the category of gender considers power not as an absolute static being, but as a conjunction of forces that moves among/against/over/with the various social actors. It is therefore an analysis of the circulation of power[6] in a specific social structure. Considering that androcentric knowledge and patriarchal power present in diverse theological contents are not exclusive property of the University, but rather a reality that cuts across and overcomes the many manifestations of culture, this reflection does not pretend to deal with knowledge as that which is sexist. This would mean, at the very least, a generalization and intransigence in dealing with other realities and social constructions as if they were exempt from this mark.

In the light of that knowledge which is androcentric in character, the concept of social gender relations[7] is presented as a new paradigm capable not only of making women and other oppressed groups visible, but also of illuminating the discoveries concerning the structure of the oppression and the power plays that organize normative discourses and establish social controls in the realm of the production and transmission of knowledge.

We are not proposing gender as the only, or even the best of paradigms, but rather underline its strong contribution, evident today in scientific and academic productions in various areas of knowledge.[8] Gender theories have their significance for and contribution to the analysis of human and social relations, the construction of knowledge, the process of knowledge transmission and collective construction in the academic environment, research and university extension for its inter/trans disciplinary dialogue, as well as for debating processes of participation in realms of power.

This reflection assumes a theoretical and methodological position that results in a break with the pretensions toward neutrality in the production of knowledge or in hermeneutics. The current reading of the institutional process is not without presuppositions and influences from the context from which the interpretation proceeds, neither are other readings with which this research establishes dialogue and confrontation.

The theoretical framework containing the concept of an actor who chooses the object and the working method reaffirms neutrality as a myth.[9] It also brings to the fore a questioning of a pure objectivity for studies that affirm that the only conceivable objectivity is one that is situated. Besides being dated, sexist, and racist, it implies eliminating the duality of subject-object, objectivity-subjectivity, rationality-emotivity, public-private, personal-political, etc., as well as questioning the gender, universal and temporal character of hermeneutics and knowledge.

Based on these presuppositions of the contextualization of objectivity in the analytical task, it is not strange to admit subjectivity as a part of the method, while avoiding the fallacy of a production of knowledge that is capable of attaining totalizing and absolute concepts. An objective-subjective dynamic implies the assumption that whoever produces knowledge imprints on it his or her personal conditioning and commitments with reality; therefore, the selection of the object, method and categories carries that mark. It is still necessary to point out that admitting subjectivity does not mean to assume a total relativization of the methods and results. It does not mean, either, for each to say what they think nor of legitimizing any specific type of interpretation. We admit here that subjectivity is a part of the method and is integrated into the scientific arsenal that makes possible the analysis and production of knowledge.

We organize our research on the basis of feminist theoretical constructions that find in the theories of gender a contribution to the studies of social power relations that permeate human and social relations as well as the production and transmission of knowledge. Socially and historically constructed situations can therefore be deconstructed, constructed and reconstructed based on new foundations and criteria.

These reflections on the composition of the method, although brief, are without a doubt important for overcoming the idea that we can go to the texts to be analyzed without intentions, suppositions, and analytical tools. The possibility of arriving at any kind of interpretation that is exempt from such a presuppositionally filled construction of methods in this reflection denies the reality of what the author brings to the process.

2. Gender and Latin American Feminist Theology

Before mentioning the use of the categories of gender in theology, we will briefly mention the history of feminist theology in Latin America to locate within it the category of gender. Periodization concerns itself with the experience of theology in the last three decades and divides theological developments into three different periods.[10] Each moment or period of this theology is closely related to the social, political and economic reality of the Latin American context and connected to an interaction with the discoveries and challenges experienced by groups of women and the feminist movement. One movement does not necessarily improve on or eliminate the previous one. Rather, they exist as different perspectives and tendencies within the same feminist Latin American theology.

The first moment of feminist theological reflection was in the 1970s. It was characterized by the discovery of the face of women as a specific face within the world of the poor. They cry of women for dignity and respect sounded out with other cries that made themselves heard through the Theology of Liberation. The context of poverty, of the denouncing of injustices, of commitment to offended and disrespected human dignity in the face of the poorest identifies feminist theology in this first moment, but continues to appear in the following moments.

The 1980s witnessed greater insertion of women into the academic theological world, with increasing numbers present in theological institutes, seminaries, and universities. This marks a second moment in the reflection of feminist Latin American theology. Theological production concentrated on recuperating the feminine dimensions of God, in a complementary relationship with patriarchal theology. For this reason some identified themselves as doing "theology from a woman's perspective" or "women's theology." The first moment of feminist theology lacked theoretical instruments that would allow a reading of the relationships that are classified today as gender relationships, within the traditional class analysis. The second moment, in which the feminine attains greater visibility, does not identify the differences and the relationships of domination as social constructions, but rather uses an essentialist analysis with respect to the construction of a feminine and masculine identity and the relationship between them.

Theological reflection from a gender perspective, which we identify as the third moment of feminist theology on the Latin American continent and in the Caribbean, arises in the 1990s and positions us in a broader conceptual framework. Not only does it question power relations in theological production, but also "inserts theology in a holistic, systematic and ecological paradigm."[11] This new place of feminist theology does not involve only a new theological perspective. Upon unmasking the myth of neutrality,[12] as well as the concepts of scientific objectivity, impartiality and universality that are present in the basis and structure of patriarchal thought and theological production, feminist theology from the perspective of gender categories carries out the task of deconstructing theology in which the hermeneutics of suspicion receive new nuances and strength. Some themes have stood out in the development of this theology.

Theology of and in the quotidian (every day life): The affirmation of situated objectivity as the only means of constructing knowledge ratifies the importance of the quotidian (every day life) as a theological place. Situated objectivity implies, as we say previously, the elimination of dualities such as subject-object, rationality-emotivity, public-private, personal-political, etc. Every day life arises as a hermeneutical category that makes possible the overcoming of this dichotomized view of life. In the quotidian, feminine and masculine identities, resulting from social construction, break with imposed and accepted cultural patterns. Every day life is the place for the building of new relations that affirm the dignity and human life of women and men.

Theology of the flesh, the spirit, and desire: To admit to subjectivity as part of the production of knowledge is to recuperate the place of the body, feminine and masculine, in doing theology. This affirmation reveals the fallacy of the existence of neutral knowledge that pretends to be disembodied and therefore universal. In Latin American feminist theology, the body is present in many ways. It is present in the cry against the violence suffered by women, violence that humiliates and kills. The cry of those that could not or were incapable of crying, of those who are silenced by the force of power, is present and incarnated in our cries for justice and dignity. Because we experience so much death in everyday life, we resist a theology of sacrifice. We insist on the discovery of the body as a place of joy, pleasure and the enjoyment and sharing of life, recovering celebration as a place for the manifestation of God.

Theology with flavour, warmth and affection: The patriarchal theological discourse led to the feminization and victimization of affection, allowing only women, girls, and, to some extent, boys to manifest affection. A theology that takes on the task of breaking with the gender identities assigned by patriarchalism, recovers affection as part of human life. To men who have been estranged from the possibility of loving and expressing love, it presents the challenge and the right to tenderness. Tenderness is presented as a way of being in the world and, through it, we rediscover sorority, the friendship of God with humanity. God is the friend who supports us and walks with us.[13]

Theology as a re-encounter with the universe: One of the contributions of gender theories to theology is the holistic world vision in which humanity discovers itself as part of a whole, integrated with the vital energy of nature. Eco-feminism, a theological expression developed in the last few years,[14] focuses on the holistic dimension of theology. Eco-feminism in Latin America reaffirms the fundamental elements of ancestral Indigenous, Afro-

Latin American and peasant ("campesino") theologies.

Pluricultural theology: The space, that is opening as a result of gender theories, has enabled the recognition of the ethnic and cultural differences in Latin America and the Caribbean. We are a diverse Latin American continent and that diversity is expressed in a plural feminist theology. Theology from the perspective of indigenous women recovers, above all, their relationship with mother earth. It contrasts with man's attitude of possession of the earth, which has meant social exclusion, violence, and death of their forefathers and culture for indigenous peoples. Their theology recovers the dimensions of the care, respect and responsibility of humanity for nature. Black feminist theology has recovered the relationship with the ancestors as part of their theology. It is a tradition that maintains a close relationship with nature. In some of its expressions, the divinity lies in the rivers, stones, mountains and waterfalls, in the wind and in the sea. They are places of worship and of meeting God. This relationship of belonging to a larger body that welcomes me results in an attitude of service and responsibility for creation. Both theologies struggle against racism, are critical in the face of ethnocentric and exclusionist Christian theologies, and have insisted on the importance and urgency of inter-religious dialogue as a relevant theme for current theological reflection.

Conclusion

This brief overview of Latin American feminist theology has allowed us to open the doors to understand a little more about current thinking and events, on the Latin American continent, having to do with this topic. In conclusion, we would like to mention three elements that are present in this article which we want to emphasize.

The first is the topic of masculinity. This has also been a contribution of gender theories that very slowly is being taken up by men. We believe that as they become interested and deepen this subject, it will become an important space for dialogue and mutual enrichment.

The second element concerns the relationship among theology, gender and feminism. The Latin American theologians represented here identify ourselves as feminist theologians. We understand feminist theology not only as a contribution to the feminist movement, but also as a form of feminist militancy. The gender theories are a reference, a set of theoretical tools that are added to other tools of analysis. We do not refer to a theology of gender, but rather to the use of gender analysis by feminist theology.

In conclusion, we go back to the beginning. The founding principle of theology in Latin America and the Caribbean is that it arises "from the world of the impoverished." We are convinced that the harsh reality of neoliberal globalization calls us to stand strong in an attitude of constant defense of life and of a life of dignity for the excluded. The feminization of poverty is part of the harsh reality of our continent and it jumps out at us in a clear, open manner. That is why our words will always carry with them the strains of blood of the victims and will be accompanied with the commitment to end violence and injustice. It will always be a far cry for and of freedom!

Notes

1. Sallie McFague, *Modelos de Dios – Teologia para una era ecologica y nuclear* (Santander: Sal Terrae, 1987), pp. 259-299.

2. See: Ivonne Gebara, *Intuiciones ecofeministas, ensayo para repensar el conocimiento y la religion* (Montevideo: Doble Clic Soluciones editoriales, 1998).

3. The expression "generally" used here refers to the social relations of gender, and in this context, to the construction of identities, roles, functions and relations attributed socially to men and women.

4. Maria Jose F.R. Nunes, "Estudios feministas e elaboracao teologica" in *Sao Bernardo do Campo*. Instituto Metodista de Ensino Superior, 1991, p. 6 (mim).

5. Cf. Heleieth I.B. Saffioti, "Rearticulando genero e classe social" in Albertina de Oliveira Costa e Cristina Bruschini, *Uma questao de genero*, Rio de Janeiro: Rosa dos Tempos, 1992, pp. 197-199; Joan Scott, *Genero: uma categoria util para a*

analise historica, Recife: SOS-Corpo, 1991, pp. 14-17.

6. Verify Foucault's concept of power in the discussion of gender theories by Heleieth Saffioti and Joan Scott. cf. Heleieth I.B. Saffioti, *op.cit.*; Christina Bruschini, *op.cit.*; and Joan Scott, *op.cit.*

7. Cf. Scott, Saffioti, and Bruschini, *op.cit.*

8. Albertina de Oliveira Costa and Cristina Bruschini, *Uma questao de genero*, Rio de Janeiro: Rosa dos Tempos, 1992; Scott, *op.cit.*; Sheyla Benhabib and Drucilla Cornell (coord.), *Feminismo como critica da modernidade, releitura dos pensadores contemporaneos do ponto de vista da mulher*, Rio de Janeiro: Rosa dos Tempos, s/d.

9. Cf. Hilton Japiassu, *O mito da neutralidade cientifica*, Rio de Janeiro: Imago, 1981, p. 35.

10. On the periodization of Latin American Feminist Theology, see Ivonne Gebara, "Aportes para una teologia feminista, in *Topicos* 90, Chile, 1993, pp. 71-133. On the same subject, but focusing on feminist hermeneutics, see Elsa Tamez, "To be fully human...EATWOT women's theologies", Ecumenical Association of Third World Theologians, Manila, 1998.

11. Yoland Ingianna, "Teologia, liberacion y paradigma de genero: appuntes en marcha para la reflexion colectiva" in *Vida y pensamiento*, Vol. 14, No. 1, 1994. Seminario Biblico latinoamericano, San Jose, Costa Rica, p. 51.

12. Cf. Hilton Japiassu.

13. Sallie McFague, *Modelos de Dios – Teologia para una era ecologica y nuclear* (Santander: Sal Terrae, 1987), pp. 259-299.

14. Cf. Ivonne Gebara.

Culture/Gender in Latin America

Diego Irarrazaval

In our reality, there are intense opinions about the human condition, contested discussions about gender and culture, and a quest to clarify paradigms. I begin in an unconventional way: my own longing and anguish about being human.

My Concerns

Abstract language about being human is often arrogant and meaningless. So I prefer to share with you questions and suspicions about my personal and theological condition. Otherwise I may mislead you and also deceive myself.

For several decades, I have done theology in dialogue with religions and cultures of common people. Why? Because I do not feel at home with mainline Christianity, which is mono-cultural and mono-religious. Moreover, I deeply enjoy "other" forms of life and faith that are characteristic of Latin American peoples. Perhaps my fascination with the "other" is due to my spiritual shortcomings.

Moreover, it hurts me, and hurts others, to see that liberation theology is often removed from the everyday life of people and from their feelings and spirituality. Why don't we take into account everyday longing for liberation?

Concerning gender, today I am appalled by patriarchal styles of Christianity. I ask why I became concerned about it after turning fifty years old. How can I deal with the notion of gender being unmarried and within a community of male religious? What is gender, in the Andean region (Bolivia, Peru, Ecuador, and sections of neighbour-nations) where I live, with its peculiar correlation between masculine and feminine dimensions? Furthermore, I am challenged by feminist theology. It shows, among other things, that much of my work and feeling is unilateral and rude.

Anguish and suspicion overwhelm me. Will I be able to live, pray, and think, with a healthy gender perspective? When I do envision and practice this point of view, it seems that I do attain more personal freedom, deeper relationships, and new ways of doing things. At the same time, we continue to seek strategies to eliminate gross discriminations in society and in the church. This is a burdensome task.

Communities throughout the Latin American continent are recreating their understanding of the faith. Let us consider, for example, Basic Christian Communities in Brazil, which have held national meetings since 1975.[1] However, only since 1992, did they begin to consider cultural, religious, and gender issues of the common people. Obviously, there have been mistakes within these communities, and also great deficiencies among us theologians who work in their midst.

Much is yet to be done. Theological discourse has to take into account everyday human needs and common wisdom. In Latin America, there is hardly any dialogue about art, ecology, the reality of youth, cultural conflicts, gender, and religious and spiritual developments, in short, dialogue with "lo cotidiano" throughout our continent. Yet, these realities should be more present in our theological work.

As we relate to God, and ponder on revelation and salvation, we need to unfold this process in contextual and concrete ways.

This implies that theologically we be nurtured by the cry of the people; namely, by cultural, political, gender, emotional, economic, ecological, and other manners in which people cry for life. We also theologically confront globalization, which rests on economic and cultural absolutes. Moreover, within communities in Brazil and in other regions, theology includes a critique of the totalitarian market with its secular myths and rituals. In a positive sense, many communities contribute to the reconstruction of the social fabric and interpersonal relations.

I also wish to be set free from a host of chains. Many of us feel like we are in prison, because we are chained to androcentric models, modern conceptual dualisms, postmodern skepticism, intolerance, subtle and widespread forms of fundamentalism, and lack of imagination and courage. These terrible chains hinder our faith and theologies. Even when our practice derives from a desire for liberation, we still become entangled and trapped.

For example, the poor are often treated in unilateral terms as economic and socially impoverished. Undoubtedly, they are victims of unjust structures. But the poor also have cultural, psychological, racial, gender and other basic characteristics. A similar shortsighted approach is used in gender analysis; for instance, when "woman," "man," "sex," "gender," "power," "relationships" etc., are not dealt with in all their complexity.

There is also a need for substantial critique of what is said to God (our spiritualities) and what is said about God (our theologies). One is disturbed by certain Christian theologies that behave as if they have ownership over the sacred. They pretend to define God. However, Jesus spoke of the Kingdom through parables; God has given no definition to mystery! To "explain transcendence" is an impossible dream. We may only contemplate, enjoy, and be co-creators with God, who saves humanity from the illusion of being gods.

Gender sensibility impels us to be careful in theological language.

The divine presence may not be reduced to ethnocentric masculine and feminine categories. God is not a Western deity; nor simply Father and Mother. Franz Hinkelammert invites us to be prudent; language about God has a human content, and theology that "uses language about heaven necessarily speaks about earth."[2] The Christian tradition gives witness to an incarnate and paschal presence of God. The sacred is not a heavenly entity. In my experience, I am fascinated by Andean Christianity with its "earthly spirituality."[3]

Ernesto Cardenal, Nicaraguan poet and politician, speaks of humanity, man and woman, as representatives of creation, and as "seeds of new seeds."[4] I also see human beings as part of creation, where women and men interact. Within creation we feel God's endearing presence. In such terms one may better understand human and cosmic realities.

Debate Over the Human Condition

Scientific work and theological discourse include dialogue and confrontation. When we consider the plurality of Latin American cultures and their manners of understanding the sacred, we are led to discuss ethnocentric and mono-cultural forms of speaking about God. Moreover, a gender perspective helps us to uncover power games that have an impact in sacred images.

What human dialectics are prominent in Latin-America? Let us examine the dominant and the alternative understandings of being "subjects" or human persons.

The dominant way of thinking is dualistic and it excludes the "other." Subject and object are seen one against the other; objects are instruments in the hands of an omnipotent subject. Likewise, nature and culture, body and spirit, the individual and society, tradition and modernity, are all seen in terms of a dualistic pattern. We have the problem not only of dichotomies but also of exclusions. Modern cultures scorn traditional ones. The masculine sees itself as superior to the feminine (and marginalizes its meanings). These points of view are embedded in economic-cultural totalitarian structures, which disregard other economic and cultural forms of life. The dichotomy of subject-object has been transferred to the Creator as subject and to the world as object. At the same time, patriarchal features are attributed to God.

These perspectives are implicit in most theological discourses. They even distort theologies that claim to go beyond the status quo. Often we understand the faith with particular, androcentric, rational, and dualistic mentalities. For example, language about God in history and about an individual-subject of faith are not universal. They belong to a particular western framework. Such languages disregard God in creation and in community; they also disregard the presence of the Spirit of non-Christian cultures and religions. Moreover, the vision of a sacred cosmos is often classified as something pagan and pre-Christian.

However, there is a different and alternative understanding of the human condition: we become subjects (in Spanish we speak of "la subjetivacion"). This process is personal, historic, and cosmic, where we encounter a divine and saving Presence. Enrique Dussel explains the Latin American condition as that of "bodily subjects who hunger for justice."[5]

A moment ago I spoke against dualisms. But an alternative framework is not monistic or totalitarian. Rather, one has to acknowledge differences, the values of a holistic approach, and the transformation of reality. Different aspects of the human condition are most important contributions to a new heaven and earth.

I must also highlight the interaction between cultures, and between the masculine and the feminine. We treasure inter-cultural dynamics between members of different cultural systems, where one does not eliminate the "other"; but, rather, one affirms oneself and the other, constructing our differences and reciprocities. This happens in some of our "mestizo" realities. Likewise, the masculine and feminine conditions, developed in particular socio-cultural contexts, become an encounter between different elements that have a common desire for humanization.

Being human, as men and as women, has specific meanings within regions of our continent. I will refer to three contexts where good research has been done on these issues. More specifically, I am interested in symbolic systems (the three I mention, and many others) that offer alternatives to dominant forms of existence.

In the Andean region, relationships are the key and all encompassing reality. This culture has no place for an isolated individual, nor for dualistic separation of the masculine and feminine, nor for mistreatment of the cosmos as if it were a mere object. Every being lives and is in relationship with the other and with the whole. Jose Estermann offers this explanation: "people are not subject in a restrictive sense . . . rather they are constituted by relationships; . . . in the sexual polarity of woman and man (that is not dualistic nor exclusive) the universe has its thicker and basic expression, especially through ritual and celebration."[6] It is evident that this human cosmology enriches our theological discourse. Instead of a static Christian truth, there exists a living truth that enhances relationships.

Nahuatl wisdom (in Mexico and Central America) is also dynamic and holistic. As it happens with other aboriginal peoples, the Nahuatl comprehends the sacred as dual and relational. Miguel Leon Portilla explains our relationship with the Divine in this way: "Mother and Father of the gods, mirror of day and night, our mother, our father, that live in a dual reality." He adds that the human person has an inner face and also a heart of relationships.[7] In other words, there is a duality of reciprocal elements, and not a dichotomy where one factor is a denial of the other. It seems to me that when this wisdom is acknowledged theologically, we may admire God's presence in the masculine and in the feminine, in motherly and fatherly dimensions of reality.

Let us also consider modern culture, as it develops among

marginal peoples in the city. Here each person has elements of the modern outlook: freedom, critical reason, pluralism, etc. At the same time, there are other elements that have a syncretic and vital character. Christian Parker has examined behaviour and belief among poor people in Chile and throughout the continent. These peoples have "another logic," a "syncretic thinking," "a body of belief and wisdom about the world, society, politics, culture, family, life and cosmos".[8] It is "another" way of being a modern person (without false absolutes).

These three symbolic systems have their specific values, and they also have a sense of co-responsibility among human beings and within the cosmos. Everything and everyone have a relationship with what is different, and a relationship to a Divine Presence that places no barriers to life.

Our Paradigms

Many persons misinterpret Latin American theology as if its only or most important concern were social transformation. Due to the option for the poor and their struggles, we do think the faith with the paradigm of justice and hope among and for all.[9] During three decades (1970-2000), different communities of faith have developed new methods for thinking the faith, for understanding love of God, nature, and humanity. Moreover, we are now challenged and inspired by a gender perspective.

The major developments in Latin America and the Caribbean regions may be summarized in the following way. The foundations have been systematic efforts (Leonardo Boff, Juan Luis Segundo, Jose Miguez Bonino, Julio de Santa Ana, Jose Comblin and others); indigenous theologies (the work of Eleazar Lopez and processes throughout the continent); Afro-American theologies (Antonio Aparecida da Silva, Silvia Regina da Silva, and others); feminist theologies (Elsa Tamez, Ivonne Gebara, Ana Maria Tepedino, Maria Clara Bingemer, Carmina Navia, Maria Pilar Aquino, and many others); outstanding biblical work (Carlos Mesters, Milton Schwantes), and women and men doing hermeneutics in different contexts.

Each person and group doing theology has special contributions in terms of epistemology. Various paradigms have been born and grown to maturity. Jon Sobrino made the proposal that theology is an "intellectus amoris;" it seems to me that the basic thrust of Latin American theologies is to ponder human love in terms of God's saving presence.[10]

Together with this basic thrust to think Christian love, there is a beautiful mosaic of faith expressions and hermeneutics. We have a gamut of theological paths and paradigms, with their mediations: spiritual, conceptual, symbolic, ecumenical, and inter-religious. One can say that our theological endeavours are pluri-cultural and inter-cultural. This is due to the creative experiences of many communities of faith; the presence of God is meaningful within different cultural, spiritual and human journeys.

Therefore, the ways of doing theology arise from not one mono-cultural androcentric subject, but rather from creative communities of faith. Latin America is not culturally/religiously homogenous. There are many forms of Christian life, of Christian thinking and action. Moreover, these are called to dialogue with other symbolic and religious movements. Since there are different human experiences of God, and a wide spectrum of communities of faith, we also have several types of theology.

In addition, the Latin American theological scenario may undergo deep changes due to the gender perspective. Is it a new paradigm? Is it another hermeneutic? Will it be one more theme added to other theological developments? No. Many of us see that it is something fundamental and multidimensional. Gender is present in all dimensions of action, feeling, power, thinking, prayer, and celebration. Gender is present in the human body and mind, and in spiritualities. It is not in a vacuum that God is experienced.

Indeed, the Gospel is lived and the Trinity is contemplated. All of this happens in terms of our being men and of being women, in terms of the masculine and the feminine gender.

So, gender is not a framework that is juxtaposed to other factors (politics, culture, economics, ecology, etc.). Nor do we simply consider, with the eyes of faith, some gender issues. Nor does one include themes that "belong to women" and their feminist theologies.

Rather, a gender vision and action take place in everyday life and in historical existence. Furthermore, it concerns men and women and persons of all cultures. In terms of theology, gender is important in the whole experience of faith and in the understanding of God's revelation and salvation. The contents of faith in Christ and of the life in the Spirit are received and put into practice by men and by women with their gender characteristics. These contents touch upon the feelings and structures of the masculine and the feminine; they inspire gender co-relationships, our historical responsibilities, and our care of the cosmos.

This may seem obvious, but it is not so. Androcentric and patriarchal stereotypes have blinded our eyes and paralyzed our hands. In our Latin American faith-communities and theological institutions, we have yet to take into account the gender perspective/action. In my own work, I have to recognize a proud and totalitarian mode of thinking the faith; for a long time I presupposed that my masculine perspective was universal. Because strong questions and criticisms were addressed to me, and because of friendship and work done with women theologians, I am now awakening to a masculine/feminine agenda.[11]

When theology is done with a gender perspective and action, it becomes possible to encounter a Merciful and Joyful Presence. This revelation of the Good News confronts our painful and violent human condition. It also fosters hope. The Beatitudes bring forth a revolution, and are a source of realistic hope. This certainly involved both women and men. It is not a property of women (nor is it of men). As men and as women, we have different attitudes and responses to the Mystery of Love; and the same time we share and are enriched by coming together in journeys of faith.

I also wish to give witness to two gifts. They belong, in the Andean context, to indigenous spirituality. It generously places its treasures in the hands of other persons. I thank the indigenous peoples for these spiritual and theological gifts.

I used to consider everyday reality and material things to be on one side, and God on another side. This has changed. It is due to my contact and conversion within the Andean way of being Christian. Life is "kawsay" (in quechua language). This life runs through and wraps up each and all being, death and life, body and spirit, cosmos and history, and humanity and God. It is not a sort of animism nor a pantheism. I thank Andean people for pointing out to me the presence of God through "kawsay."

Another precious gift is the ability to encounter and call God in deeper ways. When one participates in rituals to mother earth, it is possible to feel and adore God in nature and all of humanity. When one calls the sacred "Tatitu" (beloved Father) as Andean people do, the presence of God is closer and more intimate. Moreover, poor Andean persons share with me a spirituality of silence and of "fiesta". So prayer consists of few words and transcendental feelings. Therefore, not only knowledge, but also worship and celebration become most important in a loving understanding of God.

An androcentric pattern gives more weight to reason; a holistic and gender inspired paradigm is more open to the Joy of God.

A last word. Throughout this essay, I have underlined interaction with the "other" in terms of culture and gender. I wish that Latin American and Caribbean theologies would be more inter-cultural and inter-religious, and, that they would also be transformed by a gender perspective and action. I am convinced that both factors foster a "loving understanding of God." This strengthens our liberating and joyful paradigms.

Notes

1. See Faustino L.C. Teixeira, *Os encontros intereclesiais de Ceb's no Brasil*, Sao Paulo: Paulinas, 1996; and essays by C. Boff and others, *As communidades de base em questato*, Sao Paulo: Paulinas, 1997.

2. Franz Hinkelammert, *El grito del sujeto*, Costa Rica: DEI, 1998, p. 9.

3. D. Irarrazaval, *Un cristianismo andino* Quito: Abya Yala, 1999. See especially the first part about earthly spirituality, pp. 15-67.

4. Ernesto Cardenal, *Cantico cosmico*, Managua: Nueva Nicaragua, 1989, p. 507-549.

5. See Enrique Dussel's notes on the workshop "Problematica del sujeto en el contexto de la globalizacion neoliberal," San Jose: DEI, January 1999, p. 33.

6. Jose Estermann, *Filosofia Andina, estudio intercultural de la sabiduria autoctona andina*, Quito: Abya Yala, 1998, pp. 201 & 208.

7. Miguel Leon-Portilla, *La filosofia nahuatl, estuadiada en sus Fuentes*, Mexico: UNAM, 1983, pp. 163 & 192.

8. Christian Parker, *Otra logica en America Latina, religion popular y modernizacion capitalista*, Santigao: FCE, 1993, pp. 366-367; see also his "Cultos y religions populares en America Latina. Identidades entre la tradicion y la globializacion," *Allpanchis* 52 (1998), pp. 239-277; and "Identity and diversity in urban popular Catholicism," in T. Bamat and J.P. Wiest, *Popular Catholicism in a World Church*, Maryknoll, New York: Orbis, 1999, pp. 19-55, where he concludes that popular Catholicism is a form of "resistance and transformation of processes that are globalizing urban life...through a sense of local community and identity... solidarity and justice" (p. 51).

9. The notion of "paradigm" is a framework and perspective, with its own values and actions. It can be said that a theological paradigm is a model with which one understands/transforms the person and community, society and cosmos, and images of God. J.B. Libanio is one among many who sees the paradigm of liberation theology in terms of history and praxis; see his "Diferentes paradigmas na historia da teologia," in VV.AA., *Teologia e novos paradigmas*, Sao Paulo: SOTER/ LOYOLA, 1996, pp. 41-43.

10. See my sixth chapter: "Nuestro paradigma: pensar el amor," in *Teologia en la fe del pueblo*, San Jose: DEI, 1999. The most important input is that of Jon Sobrino, who describes theology as "intellectus amoris" (*El principio misericordia*, Santander: Sal Terrae, 1992, pp. 49-50 and pp. 70-71), and Gustavo Gutierrez: "I am less concerned about the survival of liberation theology; I am more concerned

about the suffering and hopes of people to whom I belong, and especially to communicate the experience and message of salvation in Jesus Christ. This is the focus of our love and faith. Theology, however relevant, is only a means to deepen love and faith" ("Una teologia de la liberacion en el contexto del tercer milenio" in VV.AA., *El futuro de la reflexion teologica en America Latina*, Bogota: CELAM, 1996, p. 165).

11. I owe sincere thanks to many persons who are walking with me in gender sensibility, thinking, and action. In a special way, I thank the following women theologians: E. Tamez, A.M. Tepedino, I. Gebara, L. Quezada, D. Canales, M.C. Bingemer, M.P. Aquino, O. Ortega, A. Potente, and other good guides and friends. My first essays have been "Perspectiva de genero en la teologia" (published in *Boletin de ASETT*, 1, 1998, pp. 3-7); and an unpublished essay: "Si el grano de trigo muere…de maucho fruto; impugnacion de lo macho, a fin de ser un hombre cristiano" (1999). Also in terms of the masculine, see Leonardo Boff, "O masculino no horizonte do novo paradigma civilizacional" in W. Boechat (org.), *O masculine em questao*, Petropolis: Vozes, 1997, pp. 96-107.

Gender and New (Re-newed) Images of the Divine

Ana Maria Tepedino

Introduction

I want to share some experiences with groups of women in workshops on gender issues. Beginning with gender and religion, they also reflected on gender and ethics, gender and politics, gender and education, and gender and family.

The participants of those workshops were women from the grass roots communities, or militants in women's movements, or in pastoral movements inside the Catholic Church, or Christian professionals, some of them with Ph.Ds.

What they had in common was their struggle for a new identity and a new proactive posture in the Catholic Church and in society. Several were medical doctors, two of them surgeons, in a profession where women are highly marginalized.

Some of them spoke about their experiences of oppression, either in church or in society, and how hard it was to be recognized as equals to men and legitimate people in what they were doing.

In fact, they want to understand why these things happened to women. But they also perceived that the poor, the migrant, the indigenous people, the afrolatinamerican, and the young suffered the same marginalization.

So, we can say that we women, share our political situation of oppression with other subjects in society and in the churches.

When we women denounce exclusion in language in church and society, we are refuted with arguments such as: the expression "men" means humanity; it includes, man and woman. So there is no need to specify the particularity of woman. This fact shows clearly how women are made invisible under the symbol "man." In that sense, the masculine signifies the political and historical subject, the universal symbol, the norm for laws and social rules, and the paradigm for humanity.[1]

Although this situation is already changing, nevertheless, man/woman equality is a myth. And when injustice and asymmetries are recognized, the general belief is that they are due to personal difficulties, or lack of initiative, or biological incapabilities. These beliefs are part of the patriarchal behaviour which affirms that the natural basic man/woman equality is put aside and replaced by social inadequacies.[2]

We women are facing these challenges in order to build a new identity and to be recognized in our full humanity. For that purpose, we have to understand very clearly the patriarchal system in which we still live. It is an extremely negative system where hierarchical relations are established; relations of oppressor/oppressed exercised by the family father, who considers himself the master of the house, of the woman, of the sons/daughters, of workers and employees, thus creating a "kiriarchical" power in the image of the patriarchal God.[3] The expression "kiriarchical" puts us at the heart of our problem: the oppressions against women have their source in the image of the patriarchal God.

The expression "kiriarchical" comes from the Greek language

'KIRIOS' or Master; an expression applied to God. By analogy it is used to describe the family master. Consequently, the family father stands for and represents the heavenly Father.

The kiriarchical system values rationality, power, and objectivity; and all these qualities are considered to be male qualities. Women are considered emotional, irrational, subjective and passionate; and we internalize this given identity. In a society that values rationalist objectivity and cold decisions, women are taught to be secondary beings who do not know, cannot do anything alone, and should not do anything alone. In other words, we women cannot think with our own head. But since we became aware of this, a process of deconstruction of this given identity began to happen, and a new identity began to be constructed.

In groups of women and in meetings, putting together our experiences of oppression and our experience of God, we began a new path. New traces began to be drawn in the face of these new women, while we began to walk by ourselves, think by ourselves, and speak our own words, in a process of relational autonomy[4] with other women who were fighting for a new identity and men who were in search of redefining their masculinity.

In this process, women searched for an analytical mediation which could help them to understand the social relations in society.

A Look From the Gender Perspective

The gender perspective helped us to understand the social relations between the sexes which are power relations in society. While men are socialized to be political beings, women are socialized to be domestic ones. Nature does not determine this difference. Quite the opposite, culture constructs this distinction. Gender analysis helped us to understand this; relations between men/women in society are power relations. Gender is not synonymous for sex, but for sex culturally built. We are born male and female, but we become men and women according to cultural socialization.[5]

We incorporate masculine and feminine characteristics by learning behaviours, habits and ways of thinking according to social definition of what is a man and a woman. It is not nature that says the public world is for men, and the private world is for women, it is culture. From a very early age, girls are trained to be housekeepers, to care for children and to do domestic work. At the same time, boys are trained to be good workers, professionals, and to have public responsibilities. The conclusion is clear: the social division of work is a result of a cultural construction, and, consequently, it can be deconstructed.

Theology of Liberation in Latin America helped the poor; in this new way of doing theology, voiceless people were called to appear and become visible in society and churches. Among them appeared women, afrolatinamericans and indigenous people. As these three new subjects emerged, they pointed out that the socio-economic-political mediation was insufficient to explain our oppression. Culture should be considered too. And inside it, a new analytical theory, the gender analysis, surfaced as a very useful instrument.

The gender perspective facilitated an understanding of the social relations. The contradiction and antagonism central to the relations between the sexes were now relations of force which were constantly changing. This analytical perspective criticizes the myth of "the eternal feminine," an immutable condition in time and space. Moreover, it deconstructs the conception which gives different social roles to women and men. It is also a rupture with the studies which isolate women in a specific category.

Working in terms of social relations means that the two elements, men and women, are both taken into consideration, because it is the relation that makes them what they are. Studying one of the terms implies studying the other. By changing one of the terms, the other has to change too. The purpose of understanding gender issues and taking them seriously will create the possibility of constructing a new humanity. "We have to search for new ways of conviviality,"[6] "establishing alliances and nets between different subjects."[7]

Another argument for using a gender theory is that it articulates sex with class and race, for it is a hermeneutical instrument to understand the different connections between women and men. Specifically, both genders comprise of the poor, rich, indigenous afro, mestizas, mestizos, and white. Society manifests through power relations that permeate and stratify behaviours, influencing the way we women and men understand our identities. This dynamic results from the process which makes women in general (but in a special way, poor and indigenous women and mestizas, or afro descendants) dependent and marginalized.

This process not only challenges women, but it challenges men too. They feel its impact in the imagery, feel shocked by this "new" which seems to invade their universe of symbolical representations. Men's reaction is sometimes aggressive, revealing itself as rejection, violence, discrimination, and oppression. It seems to be much more difficult to men, who were socialized in a way of life of being strong, autonomous, and powerful. However, others try to hear this "new" and open themselves to his humanizing experience, answering positively and, in their acceptance, they get transformed.[8] Those who try it discover new possibilities of happiness. It is a "metanoia," a conversion, a revolution in the most inner part of themselves. Such a multidimensional proposal, rich and complex, engenders a new possibility of inter-human relations, which will create a new world order. So, it is a political proposal too.

The gender category enables women to demythologize the "myth" of the feminine nature, *deconstructs* the image created for them by the kiriarchical system, and *constructs*, and *engenders* a self image that allows them a full citizenship. Also, the gender analysis challenges men to deconstruct their identity created by the same cultural system which dehumanizes them too, and, at the same time, it engenders a new masculinity which will entitle them to live human dimensions they have ignored until now.

This new woman and new man will be able to build a new world of gender democracy[9] based on the respect for the diversity of human persons; here different does not suggest deficiency but equivalency. In addition, this attitude is articulated in the way we experience and speak about God.

Our Image of God

The man, the masculine, understands himself as the image of God, because the Jewish-Christian tradition, established in a patriarchal and androcentric context, presented the divine in an anthropomorphical way as masculine. That is why the male qualities are attributed to God: strength, power, omniscience, and controlling everything. He is the King of Kings, the Master of Masters. His son incarnates in the man, Jesus of Nazareth, and, consequently, the majority of Christians experience God as masculine, according to the characteristics attributed to men.

The masculine and patriarchal image has serious consequences:

- It legitimates and reinforces the social patriarchal structures in family, churches and society.
- It justifies the androcentric world view in relation to men's superiority and to women's inferiority; thus the masculine becomes sacred.
- It enables men to play the role of God, as his representatives in the world.
- It presents women as dependents and sinners.
- It denies women the experience of having their sexual identity affirmed as God's image, diminishing in them dignity and self-esteem.
- It reduces the divine Mystery to the metaphor of the dominant male (Patriarch). This image of God is an idol, a

source of injustice and slavery for women, the poor, the Afros, and indigenous peoples.

The patriarchal culture built this image of God, which resulted in a disaster for us, that is, women, the poor, the Afro, and the indigenous. But we can change, transform and deconstruct it. Images can be changed. Science, technological progress, communication, and our own experiences can alter our vision of the world. Our image of God can be "cured" by a different way of naming the divine presence in our life.

We feel the Mystery in another way,[10] as more interconnected in our daily lives. We feel it in ourselves, in our bodies, in the others, in nature, and in the whole cosmos.[11]

The importance of thinking about this theme is that it enables us to understand how our way of seeing the world and the relations between persons (ethics) depend on the images and stereotyped ideas we have learned. The vision of the cosmos produced by patriarchy created a theological conception which provoked a specific behaviour. For instance, the masculine is the image of God and women are not, because they are second range beings. And, in a parallel manner, women are esthetically worse, because they sinned first and led men to sin. The foundation for this interpretation is a wrong hermeneutical perspective of Gen. 2 and 3. This mental elaboration of God legitimizes the way masculine and feminine operate in society.

In order to change this reality, the gender insight utilizes a methodological principle of deconstruction of this negative theme, by posing critical questions such as: where are the power relations in society, their impact on the definition of the women's reality, and who do they benefit? Using the hermeneutic of suspicion with relation to traditional theology, we analyze critically anthropology, ecclesiology, christology, soteriology, ethics, and spirituality.

After the deconstruction, we elaborate a critical reconstruction by redefining the theological terms, departing from the old gender perspective, and searching for a biblical-theological foundation for an alternative learning and practice. Here we consider the body, interdisciplinary approaches, the committed spirituality, and the reality of daily life (*lo cotidiano*),[12] in order to allow people to realize theological and social changes.[13]

To incorporate the gender perspective as key, inside the theological and ecclesial world is an educational effort committed to the recuperation of the true meaning of Christian faith, which bring plentifulness of life to women and men (cf. John 10:10).

New (Re-newed) Images of the Divine

In the groups I mentioned earlier in this essay, I worked with several images, in order to carry out the deconstruction of the traditional images that we have internalized and to reconstruct new ones which are meaningful to our lives today (that is, images that are easier to be understood and that speak to our present experience).[14] Then, I asked the question: which images do not express God to you and what images help you to feel and experience God?

All the groups rejected the portrayals of suffering and institutional images: stereotyped depictions of priests and sisters, the spiny crown, martyrdom, and the cross with a tortured figure. On the other hand, they welcomed symbols of love relationships (such as man and woman together), symbols of life (such as grapes, wheat, and bread and wine), symbols of light (such as the candle), and symbols of the path (such as the way). These images of love, life, light and path have always been symbols of the divine. But they have a re-newed meaning today.

The Divine is found in the daily reality of wheat and grapes which give us bread and wine, the basic symbol for living. Nobody can live without food, without meaning, without dreams, without love, without interconnections, and without interrelatedness. These images point anew to metaphors which speak about the Mystery.

The reconstruction of new metaphors to speak about the Divine comes through our experience, not only as individuals, but as groups. So we discover several images to express the Mystery. It is not primarily a rational construction, but the fruit of a deep experience, inside ourselves, in our daily life and in our history. We feel God in another way as a Mystery inside and outside us, and interconnected with our life and with all kinds of life.[15] We feel love, intimacy, and interconnectedness and we want to express this experience in a distinct way with other colours, other manifestations, and other music.[16]

We are challenged to express the Saving Presence in our current reality. God is much more than the masculine and the feminine. The Johannine community experienced, reflected, and affirmed: God is Love (1 John 4:6). And this reality was transformed in the Patriarchal father!

Every day people in their wisdom say God is "more, the great." This can be found in other religious traditions as follows: "I do not designate its name, I designate it by the term 'Word' (Tao), making violence to the concept I would say it is 'the Great.' It is here and it is there, but being there, it's still here."[17]

The verb "is" and the adverb "more" seem to express meaning much better than a noun. A noun seems to enclose the Mystery; however, we cannot enclose the Mystery. Saint Catherine of Siena compared the Mystery with the sea. The more we enter into it, the more we feel it.

This Saving Presence is interpreted as non-hierarchical, inclusive, and a de-stabilizing vision of plentifulness for all beings and creation.[18] For example, Sallie McFague reflects on the image of the divine as Mother, Lover and Friend. She explains that these metaphors are more adequate for today, because they consider the power of love, and express better the articulation of unity and interdependence. God as mother does not want to speak about the reverse of the coin of God as Father, but this metaphor attempts to build a new metaphor that can bring balance and help to create a new image for Father too. Mother means engendering, giving birth and nurturing, which are neglected factors in the Christian tradition. Although in the Bible, in the Patristic theology, and in medieval piety, God is sometimes pictured with feminine features.[19] Speaking of God as mother not only means these already mentioned characteristics, but it also underscores the fight for life, the protection for all menaced life. Therefore, it is an image connected to justice too.

In our experience with women from the popular classes, we find mothers who are the head of the families and who fight as lionesses for their children, and not only for them, but for better living conditions for all sons and grandsons in their communities.[20] The Divine Mystery seems to empower them to go on struggling. McFague calls our attention to that fact that some texts present maternal love as including the fight to protect the sons and the fight for justice, which, in general, is considered a male trait. So, she asserts that God as Mother is a vigorous image for talking about the interrelation of all life. This becomes a central sensibility in a holistic comprehension of Christian faith in an inclusive vision of plentifulness. The metaphors that explain the Mystery never can express its full reality.

In the past twenty years in Latin America, we reflected on God as the Master of History, and that image helped us in our commitment to struggle to transform society. But, now, we turn to a more holistic, inclusive and non-hierarchical one. In that sense, we can accept the image of Mother as expressing this moment in which we are living.

This model takes us closer to a different perspective on the origin of life. Here the world is not conceived as the work of the artist, but is pictured as engendering, giving birth and nurturing. This portrayal expresses the creation as deeply dependent on the divine life. In this image the world is revealed as the Body of God. What other image could express better, the basic reality of life: that we live and move and have our being in God?[21] The immanence of the divine is articulated closely with its transcendency. Feeling the intimacy with the mystery inside us and the power of the transcendency empower us to live, to love, to dream, to fight, to work and to face the challenges of our time.

This image suggests some very important consequences. The first is a new way to speak about God's love as engendering, nurturing, defending, and always taking care of the children, thereby looking for the best for them. This model of Divine Presence privileges love, intimacy, interconnectedness,[22] and resemblances between God and the world, and it helps to overcome the subordinating distinction between spiritual and biological and between women and men. This image points to an ethic of care – the attitude of preoccupation, responsibility, and affection between human beings and all creation.[23]

Conclusion

Sallie McFague compared "our theological constructions with 'houses' good to live in for a certain time, with windows partially opened and doors partially closed; they become prisons when they do not allow us to go and come, to build another room or to diminish or if necessary to build a new house."[24]

We discovered that the new images referring to the Divine are old ones, but the accent is different. Our times and our contexts help us to express this reality as we stress other colours to paint this reality where we move and have our being. The Divine mystery is inside us and outside us, in nature, and in all creation. And it inspires us to live a relation of mutual love and it empowers us to live loving relations among ourselves, the other, and the world. This other way of feeling the Divine assists people to create and re-create themselves, to cure the other who suffers, to recreate nature who is damaged, to create new relationships among persons and peoples, to dare to dream, and to have visions for a new world order. Our world is thirsty for the Divine Presence. And, without attitude of solidarity, tenderness and firmness, we are challenged by our faith to manifest this sacred revelation.

So, my hope is that this new way of naming the Sacred, this new construction of an image of the Mystery – which interconnects human experience, spirituality, social, ecological and theological expressions and new possibilities for interhuman relations – will open creative avenues to forge a new world.

Notes

1. Cf. Simone de Beauvoir, *Le deuxieme sexe*, Paris, 1948.

2. Cf. Marcela Lagarde, "Identidade de genero y derechos humanos," in *Una Mirada feminista en el umbral del milenio*, Instituto de Estudios de la mujer, Universidad Nacional Heredia, Costa Rica, pp. 42-48, here p. 42.

3. Cf. Elisabeth Schussler Fiorenza, "Ties that bind: domestic violence against women", in *Voices from the Third World*, vol. XVIII, no. 1, June 1995, pp. 122-167, here p. 165, note 2.

4. This expression is quoted in Margarida Brandao, "Teologia na perspectiva da mulher", in M. Fabri dos Anjos (org.) *Teologia aberta ao futuro*, Soter, Paulinas, 1997.

5. Cf. Gayle Rubin, *The Traffic on Women, Notes on the Political Economy of Sex*, 1975, a book that provides the framework for the theory of a Gender perspective.

6. Cf. Ivone Gebara, *Teologia ecofeminista*, Sao Paulo, 1997, pp. 10-12.

7. Cf. Diego Irarrazaval, "Si el grano de trigo muere...da mucho fruto-impugnacion de lo macho: a fin de ser hombre cristiano", a paper presented at the IV Latin American meeting on feminist theology, Bogota, Colombia, August 1999.

8. Cf. *Ibid*.

9. Cf. Marcela Lagarde "identidades de genero e Direitos Humanos" in *Una mirada feminista en el umbral del milenio*, Instituto de Estudios de la mujer, Universidad Nacional Heredia, Costa Rica, 1998, pp. 42-84.

10. Cf. Consuelo del Pardo, "Yo siento a Dios de outra manera", in Elsa Tamez (org.) *El rostro femenino de la Teologia*, Dei, Costa Rica, 1987.

11. Cf. Final document, in A.M. Tepedino and M.P. Aquino (eds.) *Entre la indignacion y la esperanza, Teologia feminista Latinoamericano*, ASETT/Indo-American Press, 1998, pp. 197-211; Final Document, "Violence on Women:

Spirituality for Life", in *Voices from the Third World*, June 1995.

12. The importance of daily life was presented by Agnes Helles, *Sociologia de la vida cotidiana*, Peninsula, Barcelona, 1977; cf. Ada Maria Isasi Diaz, *En la lucha*, where she demonstrates the importance of the daily life to the way women theologize; see also Ivone Gebara, *Teologia ecofeminista*, Olho d'Agua, Sao Paulo, 1997, p. 12.

13. Cf. Final Document, Encuentro Pedagogia, "Teologia y Genero" in *the II Encuentro-Taller de Profesoras de Teologia*, Managua, Nicaragua, enero 2000.

14. Like playing cards or man/woman together, a book (the Bible), a candle, the letters alpha and omega, a priest, a nun, a martyr (San Sebastian) a spiny crown, a bunch of grapes, a cross with a tortured figure, a crown with a lamb, an angel, bread and wine, a boat with a cross, a pigeon, wheat, etc.

15. Ivone Gebara, *Rompendo o silencio*, Vozes, 2000, pp. 232-235, where she proposes the expression "Zoe diversity", meaning Life in all its richness interconnected with all expressions of the living mystery.

16. Cf. Idem, *Teologia em rimo de mulher*, Paulinas, Sao Paulo, 1993.

17. Cf. Lao-tze on *TAO TE KING* 24/1-3 and 51/4.

18. Cf. Sallie McFague, *Modelos de Deus, Teologia para uma era Ecologica e Nuclear*, Sao Paulo, 1996, p. 117.

19. Cf. Ibid., p. 144.

20. Cf. Tereza Maria Pompeia Cavalcante, "Relatorio do VI Intereclesial das Comunidades de Base" in *REB* 1987.

21. Cf. Acts 17:22.

22. Cf. Ute Seibert, "Dios: Poder en relacion", in *Cons-pirando* 16, junio 1996, pp. 40-43.

23. Cf. Leonaardo Boff, *Saber cuidar*, Petropolis, 1998, p. 11.

24. Cf. S. McFague, op. cit., p. 49.

The Shifting Gender Role of Women

Judith Na Bik Gwat

The gender role is always limited to a particular location and time. This means that the gender role in one area is different from another area. In fact, the role of gender in one place may even be different in the past, present and future. Therefore, in this paper I analyze my observation on the gender role of women in their leadership on Sulawesi Island of Indonesia. As I consider this region, it has many unique features. I therefore explore a small part of the Sulawesi hinterland. I have observed a distinctive gender role in the southern part of the Sulawesi mountains (particularly in the area of Toraja), in Central Sulawesi (more exactly in the Lore valleys), and in the tip of North Sulawesi (around the Minahasa mountains). I will start with my survey on the gender issue in Sulawesi by moving from the South to the North, while occasionally comparing it with my origin from Java.

During my journey and observation, especially when I was in touch with the women from Sulawesi, I found that many Sulawesian women participate in the public world. This is very different from where I was brought up, in Central Java. In Java, the women's role in the public arena generally is at the market, as a breadwinner for their families. Very seldom can a Javanese woman be a village leader. While in Sulawesi, there are female village leaders, priestesses, and synod chairwomen. The public role of women as organizers in some parts of Sulawesi raises a question: why is it that the women in this region can join in the realm that is generally dominated by males in Indonesia? Although women worked for decades in the bureaucracy levels in Indonesia, one never found a clear statement that there was no place for women. However, in fifty-five years, there has never been a single woman sit as a president, a governess, or a regent. This similar situation exists at the administrative unit/sub-district position (an office which is not elected by the people) that represents the central government. Yet, a village leader is chosen by its people, so that there is still an opportunity for women to sit in that position, even though women make up only about 2% of the total village leaders in overall Indonesia.

Regarding the declining political role of women in Indonesia, Saskia E. Wieringa explains the dynamic shift in the status of women's organizations relative to men, from the political struggle to social organizational matters.[1] Owing to that, it seems the men discourage the women from entering politics, even though president Sukarno had admitted that Indonesia would not succeed without women's participation. However, many more people opposed his idea. Women's organizations began to exit from politics after the regime of Suharto, particularly when this government banned Gerwani (the Indonesian Women Movement), jailed many Gerwani executives, and accused them of being communists. During the era of Suharto's leadership for 31 years, women's organizations were transformed into wives' organizations. And, consequently, women were represented as housewives, as a husband's other half, and also as extra breadwinners. The women have never become the heads of families in the course of the bureaucratic government of Suharto.

But let us return to the Sulawesi women who are actively involved in leadership outside of governmental and bureaucratic positions. Apparently, this is because the female leaders are not considered a taboo in the traditional communities in Sulawesi. This assumption drove me toward a further search. During my investigation, I found some acknowledgment of former church leaders who still know their old traditions. For instance, before foreign influences, such as Moslem and Christian, entered and affected the culture in Sulawesi, there were indeed some female ritual leaders in the Minahasa, Lore, Pamona, Toraja and Mamasa ethnic groups. Lore, in fact, had a female ritual leader and they also had Pekasele, the queen. Minahasa had female Walian, Pamona had Tadumburake, Toraja had Tominaa Baine and Toburake,[2] and Mamasa had Tomakada. The following are examples of three regions in Sulawesi.

Torajan Women in South Sulawesi

In the traditional community, the ritual leaders generally have powerful influences in their community. The ritual leaders perceive themselves and are perceived by others as having the ability to communicate with the other world, with the spirits of their ancestors, and they also can read natural signs/omens. They are usually well versed in their pedigree, myths and folk tales, and language of prayer. Therefore, they influence or, in other words, they control and shape their community members' philosophy.

Before Christianity spread, the Torajan community believed in Aluk Toraya, a belief in the ancestor spirit that is taught through mythology and ceremonies. For instance, Tominaa means a wise person who masters the literature well. These knowledgeable people usually lead various ceremonies; therefore, a Tominaa is also a linguist and a community leader. In the Torajan community, a Tominaa can be either a woman or a man. The most important factor is their mastery of the mythology and the ceremonial language. Today a female Tominaa is called Tominaa Baine. This indicates that nowadays it is a scarcity for women to become a

Tominaa in the present day gender hierarchy.

In this power structure, the woman's role in Toraja can be tracked through their myths that have become their life guidelines. Once again the myth is not similar in all places. For example, Tulangdidi in Sesean is believed to be a woman, while in the Sa'dan valley, Tulangdidi is a man. Furthermore, except for the gender of Tulangdidi, the overall stories are alike or almost alike. In the Sesean mountains the women are considered important. Until the 1970s, many rituals required a central role for the women in the ceremonies. While, in Sa'dan valley (since its 18th century contact with the Luwu' kingdom and the following of that kingdom's highborn/aristocratic structure), in fact, many men have become the formal leaders. Perhaps that is the reason they considered Tulangdidi to be a man. Nevertheless, the Sa'dan women are skilful in organizing the ceremonies, and their traditional ritual skills became a ceremony in the Christian rites. In the war against the Dutch colonialism, there were women leading the war. On that account, in the Torajan tradition, women are accepted as leaders.

Nonetheless, when the missionaries spread Christianity and fully developed the church of Toraja in 1947, at that time the Dutch priests stated firmly that according to the church rules in the Netherlands, women were not eligible to become priests. Since then, for almost 40 years, women are not allowed to lead as priests in the Christian Torajan setting, particularly in the church of Toraja. And now, there are some elder male Presbyterians who reject the existence of a priestess. They feel uncomfortable accepting a blessing from women. However, a part of the followers of Christianity can accept women's leadership because traditionally the role of women in leadership is not a taboo. Therefore, it is no wonder that some women are directly elected by their people as village leaders in Toraja. Even though it must be noted that the election is still under the influence of Torajan's feudalism, so that the women chosen generally are from the noble families.

In the Torajan tradition, the marriage system shows the woman's position to be not lower than the man's. Specifically, the marriage system in Toraja does not recognize any dowry. This means that after the wedding, a woman does not belong to her husband's family. In fact, in many cases, many husbands follow their wives' parents. Also, in a divorce case, both women and men can divorce and remarry, since the principle of marriage in Toraja is monogamous. In the past, there was a woman who had been married six times without feeling embarrassed. Moreover, though the lineage of the Torajan family is bi-lineal, most of the Christian Torajan families are now setting up a patrilineal system. This is because they consider it more modern and better. However, some families still operate under a bi-lineal system.

I did not have a chance to study directly the other parts of South Sulawesi; however, I found a note regarding Egbert Adriaan Boerenbeker's dissertation about women's power. He wrote that in the past, many women held the power in South Sulawesi, such as in Tanette, Rappang, Supa, Laikang, Luwu, Nepo, Bacukiki, Bojo, Pambuang, Soppeng, Malusetasi, Sawito, Batulapa, Kasa and Sidenreng.[3] Even in Soppeng, till the 1990s, there were still women able to tell the stories of female datu (leaders) in their region. However, in later developments, particularly with the formal system of colonial bureaucracy and in the Republic of Indonesia government, no women were able to hold power. Nevertheless, in the people's movement against land eviction, such as on Laelae island off the shore of Makassar, there are some women who head these protesting groups.

Lore Women in Central Sulawesi

For the Central Sulawesi, I focus on Lore. In this region especially, the women's role and power are considerable. Indeed, the Lore community generally still recalls the era of pekasele governance when the queen ruled as their leader. This is in spite of the fact that the Dutch government eliminated women's leadership in Lore by appointing a man, named Kabo, to be the king, thereby replacing his wife's position. Still, the pekasele, named Polite, is remembered as the last queen of the Lore region. Not only did the Dutch government prevent women from assuming leading positions (such as the pekasele positions), but missionaries who arrived during the era of the Dutch also discriminated against women and the lower caste. At that time, the missionary school only accepted students from the upper caste. And, moreover, all teachers in the missionary school were male. Though they did accept female students, they did not allow these students to continue their study after graduating from SR (primary school). Only male students could pursue studies in Pendolo. This decision to allow only males to further their education at higher levels guaranteed an all male corps of teachers.

The discrimination against women brought by the Dutch government and missionaries greatly impacted female power in Tanah Lore, thereby, altering the public role of Lore women. During my journey in Lore, I tried to interview some elder women, but they always recommended interviewing the men instead. One evening, I interviewed an elderly man who was often unable to answer my questions, consequently, his wife started explaining various issues. But her husband told her to shut up by saying, "It's not what she is asking!" The next morning, when we visited them again, his wife did not show up to meet us; she remained in the kitchen. A female colleague of mine, proficient in the local language and my helper, went into the kitchen and had a conversation with the wife, while I kept conversing with the husband. In the kitchen discussion, the wife explained that the missionaries were unjust towards the women and the lower caste. The missionary system and mode of work only supported men and the upper caste. Thus, the missionary work is the beginning of patriarchalization in the Lore community. This swift process of patriarchalization has caused a split between men and women.

For instance, a female student, who was in the first rank of her class, had been hampered by her teacher when the student desired to continue her studies. The missionary teacher said a female student must always be second to a man. As a matter of fact, many female students are very smart. Yet, as a result of the educational and missionary policies, the men, starting from the traditional leaders to the bureaucratic levels, dominate the public sphere in Pekurehua. The history of formal female leadership only remains in the memory of the elderly people.

However, many women did not remain idle after they finished their Village School in their teens (10 years). They did perform other activities usually done by girls, such as pounding rice, making cloth from tree bark, working at the fields, etc. But then, some advanced on to more professional jobs. For instance, one woman became a PIK (Persatuan Ibu Kristen/ Christian Mother Union) teacher. And at the age of 23, she married and educated all her children to be able to work independently. In fact, one of her daughters then became a teacher and also a community counsellor.

From Tana Lore emerged Augustina Lumentut, a former moderator of Central Sulawesi Christian Church (GKST). The Lumentut family comes from North Sulawesi, but she was born and brought up in Pekurehua. By coincidence, the characteristics of Pekurehua women are not much different from the Northern Sulawesian women. In the recent conflict at Poso, some GKST congregations expected the return of a female leader in the church. They even hoped Lumentut, who is in her 70s now, would come back and lead GKST.

Even nowadays, formal leadership is in the hands of men, but it seems that culturally the women still have the influence inside the families. This shifting of men into formal leadership roles more or less caused confusion among the men. For example, while women continue to be firm and resolute in their work activities, more men escape to alcohol, due to their incompetence in carrying out the new gender tasks as village leaders, sub-district leaders, and as regents. This is because in the past, the men's duty concerned going to war to defend their village, when there was an attack from another ethnic group. In addition to warfare, they were responsible for head hunting and hunting. Meanwhile, the women remained behind and kept all the affairs arranged and ordered the village.

The Minahasan Women in North Sulawesi: Strong and Sensitive

Minahasa gives birth to many priestesses. The Evangelical Christian Church in Minahasa (GMIM) has more priestesses than priests, and in the theology faculty, female students outnumber male students. However, notably the men still dominate the leadership on the Synod and Presbytery levels. Such a hierarchy exists first because of the structure inherited from the colonial church, and second because in the tradition, men can go traveling, while women are responsible for the village, just like in Tana Lore, Central Sulawesi.

The European influence in North Sulawesi had developed further than any parts in Sulawesi. Missionary Iberia had traveled to North Sulawesi around the 16th century and the intensive evangelism by Dutch missionaries started in the 18th century.[4] As a result, the gender role of Minahasan women more or less followed their matrons, i.e., the wives of missionaries and the female teachers in the schools established by the missionaries. Even given this pressure to change gender roles, it is undeniable that the indigenous women still inherited and kept some characteristics of Minahasan women from the past. For instance, as Bert Supit wrote,[5] the decision making in the family must be the outcome of a discussion between a wife and a husband. Based on the literature published, today in Minahasa, people use the Indonesian language more frequently. Nonetheless, it is not easy for the ethnic language speakers to find the gender role of women before the influence of foreign religion.

The missionary, N. Graafland, in his report to his sponsoring body, wrote about the Minahasan women, through the gender and European civilization bias which be brought to his observations. He referred to the Minahasan women as sensitive people who paid a great deal of attention to their children and families. Therefore, Graafland concluded, the responsibility of the Minahasan women towards their children is great. Regarding the general outlook of the Minahasan women, Graafland gave such comments as the following:

> The Minahasan women have strong and healthy posture, so that they can do many hard works, and they do not get tired easily. Their faces generally look fresh and they look strong. Many have good bodies, and some beautiful women among them. Healthy characteristics, clear eyes look and passionate, with thick hair.[6]

In addition, he noted the bravery of women in defending their village, while the men in Tompaso did not battle the attackers and ran away.

> When the Tompaso men escaped from the Kenilo attackers, the women took the weapons and fought back the enemies.[7]

He also noted that the women showed strength when they joined together to drag logs to erect a church in Tondano.

> Eighty women and girls dragged a long rattan that 3-4 cm thick. While sounding their cheers and gave all their efforts, they dragged heavy 80 feet long, 1 square feet thick log. They refused the men's help.[8]

The actual strength of Minahasan women as the organizers, especially in the church domain, apparently is not totally different from Minahasa mythology. For instance, Luminuut, as the first person in Minahasa, had a prayer answered and received help from a female walian, named Tareniema, who is later popularized as Karema.[9] Due to Karema answering prayer, Lumimuut became pregnant and gave birth to the first man, named Toar.

The Benefit of All these Searches

During these searches, I found a growing impoverishment and sterility of the women's spirituality, particularly in Lore. Before the missionaries explored (conquered) Lore, women became the ritual leaders. In the pre-missionary tradition, all women had a chance to become priestesses, even if only a few women were the experts and always were asked to lead the rites. However, in my effort to record the oral literature/tradition, only a few elder men were willing to share their knowledge. It is a pity that only they know the folk tales, since it is very unlikely that men will become priests; thus they do not know the prayer/ceremony language to enter the other world.

The role of the priest, which is not hierarchical and is selected naturally, is to work like the others. The priest is selected naturally in that one is asked to be a priest if one is able to articulate the prayer well and is considered able to communicate with the other world. For the context of rural churches and the churches outside Java, I find the structure of today's church, which adopted the European church-culture, to not be suitable, because the burden of the priest's financial needs is placed entirely on the congregation. As a matter of fact, a priest is not a father who has so many privileges, but a friend who accompanies the one who is in need. Perhaps it is time for the churches to learn from the model of non-hierarchical Levites, by "congregationalizing the priesthood discipleship" (*imamat am yang rasuli*). Specifically, a priest is not supposed to be a full time employee who lays an economic burden on his congregations. A capable person may serve as a priest, but his/her livelihood should be from other resources. He or she can get a job like other people.

In addition to shifting roles for priests, the church liturgy itself should be continually renewed. A particular aspect of liturgy that should be changed is the use of oppressive language in reference to God, such as only Father and Lord. These are two names used to address God that have been glued in Christians' minds and are automatically uttered out of their mouths. Yet, the concept of Lord and Father has brought about the ideology of kyriarchy and patriarchy and has impacted deeply the Christian consciousness and sub-consciousness. (As a corollary to shifting terms used to refer to God, in Indonesian churches, the matrimonial liturgy should be revised, so that the words husband and wife are no longer used.) The problem that emerges is how to expand this thinking, how to open/dismantle their minds/way of thinking that sees God as King and a Lord. God is not a King, Lord and Father, but a friend.

Experiences with the Women's Group

In the Women's Group of Awareness, named Kelompok Perempuan Sadar (KPS), I began to interpret texts by referring to the ordinary realities and experiences, which led to our principle focus on violence against women, for instance in the liturgy. However, it is not adequate to take up these reform measures in KPS only. In addition, we have to find a way to bring about renewal inside the churches themselves. The liturgy of churches requires renewal, since today's liturgy continuously fosters androcentrism. In fact, the liturgy of churches generally acts as a commemorating ceremony and in a rigid atmosphere, specially the weekly liturgy. We also need a ritual that is able to be expressed verbally or non-verbally and uses various symbols, so that the liturgy becomes beautiful, impressive and challenges creativity.

Therefore, in semester 3 (January 1998 – April 1999) of teaching liturgy in East Indonesia Seminary in Makassar, I trained students to compose liturgies based on the daily realities in their environment. I encouraged them to utilize whatever realities they were willing to bring up in the worship. We also delved into some ethnic rituals to understand how bereft of richness and meaning our church liturgy really was.

With those students, we found Kapur Sirih Pinang (lime, betel leaf, areca nut) as a common symbol in Indonesia, that still exists today from Sumatra (Borneo) to Papua and even from South Asia to the South Pacific. Kapur Sirih Pinang, often printed on the books, is rooted in our culture as a symbol of friendship, a symbol of peace, and a way of greeting. In Indonesian traditions, this symbol is still used in wedding ceremonies, particularly in the parts dealing with proposing. In these ceremonies, Sirih (betel leaf) represents a man and pinang (areca nut) represents a woman. In all traditional communities, the people chew betel together as a symbol of greeting. Chewing it also represents friendship or peace. The betel chewing ceremony no longer exists in the urban areas. But rural people are still chewing it while chatting for hours, especially during special events where many people gather. Chewing betel gives a certain pleasure, so that it smoothes the communication among the people who sit together.

Conclusion

The ongoing legacy of colonial politics and missionary work has shaped the identity of the Minahasan and the gender role in North Sulawesi, as well as in the Lore valleys in Central Sulawesi and also in Tana Toraja – South Sulawesi. For instance, the daughters of noble families could go to the village school, then they could continue their further study only in a school considered suited for girls, such as a home economics school or a teacher training school. Despite barriers placed before them, some persevering women from the teacher training schools managed to continue on to the university level. Consequently, during the era of Sukarno, a former head of Indonesia, some women received scholarships to study at overseas universities.

However, the regime of Suharto, another former political leader, framed the gender role of women as housewives and very systematically hindered women from entering politics. Nevertheless, the power of women cannot be blocked completely and oppressed absolutely. Though the state and politics so far have been coloured as a non-female world, the political situation in Indonesia became much hotter in 1999 under women's leadership. During this year, PDI, led by Megawati, won the general election. Many male politicians, then, looked for various reasons to hamper Mega, a woman, from becoming a president.

The missionary also put a distorted gender perspective into churches by claiming that women are suitable to be syamas/deacon, but not priests/ministers or a presbyter. However, the Minahasan and Lore women did not just follow the church rules of the Dutch, even though, at the synod and presbytery leadership levels, they still have to surrender leadership to men. Furthermore, from another field note of mine, I discovered that most women feel they must act like men in their capacities as leaders in order for the congregations to accept them. In fact, few women who show their gender as women in leadership also show success in solving the conflicts among the congregations.

Based on this struggle to change patriarchal structures and religious traditions, the symbols of equality and fellowship need to be developed and strengthened, while the oppressive and restraining symbols towards women need to be left out – that includes calling God a King, Lord and Father only.

Bibliography

Adriani, N., 1994, *Wanita Toraja sebagai Imam, dalam Maria Ulfah Subadio & T.O. Ihromi. Peranan dan Kedudukan Wanita Indonesia*. Yogyakarta: Gajah Mada University Press.

Boerenbeker, Egbert Adriaan, 1994, *Wanita sebagai Kepala Persekutuan Hukum Inonesia, dalam Maria Ulfah Subadio & T.O. Ihromi. Peranan dan Kedudukan Wanita Indonesia*. Yogyakarta: Gajah Mada University Press.

Graafland, N., 1994, *MINAHASA: Negeri, Rakyat dan Budayana, Jakarta: Pustaka Utama Grafiti Kaum Wanita Minahasa, dalam Maria Ulfah Subadio & T.O. Ihromi. Peranan dan Kedudukan Wanita Indonesia*. Yogyakarta: Gajah Mada University Press.

Mdatuli, Jan V. and A/P. Matuli-Walanda, 1989, *Women's Emancipation in North Sulawesi: The Story of Maria Walanda Maramis*. Kalarta: Pustaka Sinar Harapan.

Supit, Bert, 1986, *Minahasa: dari Amanat Watu Pinawetengan sampai Gelora Minawanua*. Jakarta: Pustaka Sinar Harapan.

Wieringa, Saskia Eleonora, 1999, *Penghancuran Gerakan Perempuan di Indonesia*, Jakarta: Garba budaya. Judul asil, (*The Politization of Gender Relations in Indonesia Women's Movement and Gerwani Until the New Order State*).

Notes

1. Saskia E. Wieringa, 1999, pp. 276-278.

2. In the past, there were at least three roles for priests in the Torajan community: tominaa (the wise person) led various ceremonies; toburake's main task was to communicate with the other world; and to masura' tedong (whose duty was to lead the buffalo slaughtering ceremony) was able to memorize the spell and song for the buffalo before they were slaughtered. Generally one of the tominaa's children became a tominaa since he/she often followed his/her parents who led ceremonies. Consequently, he/she knew the ceremonial language by heart.

3. Egbert Adriaan Boerenbeker, 1994, pp. 305-311.

4. Supit, 1986, pp. 7-83.

5. 1986, pp. 44-45.

6. Graafland, 1994, p. 45.

7. *Ibid.*, 1994, p. 46.

8. *Ibid.*, 1994, p. 53.

9. Supit, 1986, p. 19.

Harmonizing Masculine and Feminine in the Male Gender

Oswald B. Firth

Method as an Achievement

Men's studies impacting on gender studies is a matter of recent origin, and so far, publications on "*men as men*" have been few and far between. The reason for this, it appears, is that men's studies began from a feminist platform aimed at implementing feminist ideology and praxis.[1] There are dichotomies and contradictions in this approach as evidenced in F. Pfeil's introduction to his book *White Guys*. In an attempt to demonstrate his post-modernist research, he deconstructs his concept of the male as "a single, monolithic, absolute evil, the embodiment of white masculinity against which an interminable struggle for turf and power must be waged." But in the same breath, he reiterates that such a process of deconstruction will lead to weakening of the feminist revolutionary struggle by submitting itself to the logic of market-forces where human values are superceded by the profit motive.

Any such devaluing of revolutionary feminism, in Pfeil's view, is to be "intransigently opposed."² The logical inference one can draw from this position is that while the focus of men's studies is the critiquing and analyzing of men and their behaviour, the real purpose of such studies is to advance feminist ideology and praxis. For all intents and purposes, such an approach is clearly inadequate and fails to do justice to a correct understanding of the male gender. Any genuine study of gender must necessarily contribute to the challenge of those social, economic, political and cultural structures of domination that oppresses both men and women based on the criterion of a class struggle masquerading under the guise of gender differences.

E.A. Rotundo, in his *American Manhood* (1993), suggests that the study of gender has been derided as a woman's obsession, an intellectual plaything of feminists that would soon disappear into oblivion were it not for the political pressure it wields in contemporary society. However, one needs to acknowledge that many of our institutions have the roles of men built into their foundations. This explains why many of our behaviour patterns and thought forms have been formed by male views at specific historical points. Hence, understanding gender, especially the male gender, becomes a non-negotiable in order to understand thinking that underlie our institutions.

Dissecting the concept of male gender, social scientists have frequently documented men in sexual stereotypes as the "*Master Class*" in the modern world. Men make the laws, control the economy, and declare and fight wars.³ Privilege and power belong disproportionately to those who happen to have a penis.⁴ But male mastery does not only confer sizeable power and unmatched privileges to this particular gender, it also makes formidable demands on its members. This is because mastery is not an endowment of nature to which man has a birthright; rather, it is an art to be learnt through the combined concentration of body and mind (as demonstrated in the mastery of the Martial Arts). It is a painful process of struggle out of the weakness of boyhood into the strengths of manhood, without which the male feels he has no social recognition.

Feminism is often quick to condemn the freedom enjoyed by boys, with the connivance of their parents, when compared to the domestication of girls, as experienced frequently in indigenous rural societies in Asia. The reason latent behind such social attitudes is because society places certain stereotype expectations on boys (and on girls as well). The boys have to mature into men, assume the role of the family defender against instances of possible violence, and graduate into being the family's eventual breadwinner as the father! His father often serves as his role model. These struggles will continue until man wins his place in the world of power.[5] As for Asian girls, they are expected to guard their traditional modesty and be rooted closer to their homes. They are vulnerable and exposed to physical harassment. They are expected to behave in such a manner so that they would have an appeal as potential marriage partners in the future.

Subjectively and objectively, manhood is not simply an evolution but an achievement. The process of achievement can have its intrinsic successes and failures. The becoming of man is the struggle engaged in locating his energies between two poles of success and failure. Even if man were to earn his success as a master after much pain and enterprise, maintaining the levels of this success becomes a terribly daunting task. If he digresses and fails, sinking into depression and frustration, fall a victim to drugs and alcoholism, and become infuriated with anger and revolt, he is considered a social failure. Attempts at suicide or self-annihilation then become the escape route to permanent social rejection. R. Filene in his *Men in the Middle* provides a graphic description of the struggle to become and maintain the "*male-man*". "The yearning goes on relentlessly. Control entails self-control. Power entails will-power against weaknesses."[6]

The struggles that man faces, be they offensive or defensive, to measure up to the stereotype pushes him into the realm of doing and performing, and out of the realms of feeling and emotion. Anything that impedes the rules of success in the world of work, be they feelings of timidity, spontaneity, sympathy, or generosity, are often viewed as signs of weakness not becoming of a man.

But the 1980s began to signal that something positive and new was to happen in the lives of men. Its proponents were not notable academics or flashy TV personalities, but quiet researchers and humanistic thinkers. Among them, Robert Bly and Keith Thampson brought into focus the *Liberation of Man* which received mixed reactions. There were latent fears that positively valuing masculinity in Robert Bly's *Iron John* and Sam Keen's *Fire in the Belly* could increase men's self-esteem. Undoubtedly, this would invite accusations of promoting the worst forms of chauvinism.[7] Whatever the consequences, these works have generated avid interest among men (and even women) on the subject of male gender.

Social Construction of Gender

Manhood is not a social edict determined from above and enforced by law. Craig in *Men, Masculinity and Media*,[8] maintains that history combined with human imagination have reshaped the concept of manhood. As a human invention, mankind is used, reinforced, and reshaped by individuals in the course of human history. Based on biological differences, people of all races, places and times have invented stories about what it means to be male or female. Perceptions, therefore, of what it is to be "male" or "female" are a result of social constructs.

Plato, while discussing the ideal city, classified women and children together with men's possessions. They were the private property of men (Republic: 423e, 462e). Aristotle maintained that women are "*naturally inferior*" to men and therefore are "naturally" ruled by men. Compensation cannot wipe out or mitigate the inequality between the sexes since "political justice" can exist only between equals. Ironically and surprisingly, J.J. Rousseau, the advocate of equality and freedom, has legitimized the hierarchal divisions between the two genders on the grounds of preserving the "natural" order. Woman, he insists, is the sex that ought to obey. While granting that God has endowed both sexes with "*unlimited passions,*" man has been given reason, while woman has been given modesty in order to restrain herself.[9]

"Asian thinking," says Selvy Thiruchandran, "is in no way dissimilar to that of the West. Patriarchal minds have met. Gender ideology cuts across regions maintaining uniformity that sometimes results in parallel views being expressed through similar terminology. To cite a case in point, the Hindu lawgiver *Manu* has spoken out extensively on the superiority of men over women. Women's innate nature is considered wicked and lustful. Women, according to *Manu*, should not be entrusted with state secrets, and so, when he is consulted on important state affairs, he advises the kings to remove all women from the room as they are likely to betray high level secrets (Manu VII: 149-150). In matters of legal administration, his views are as adamant as on political affairs: "one man who is free from covetousness may be accepted as a witness, but not even many pure women because their understanding is apt to waiver" (Manu VII: 77).

Thus, relegating women to the realm of the private or the family paved the way for men to take over the functions of ordering society and gendering both family and society at large. Political theories were drawn up from this gendered state to further legitimize women's inferior position, which has resulted in the creation of an ideology of the political man and the private woman/wife.[10]

Authentic Religion and Twisted Images

The teachings of Lord Buddha sound a note of discordance with this view. Buddhism is a religion free not only from caste differences but also from gender differences. The Buddha was hesitant to accept Queen Maha Pajapati who was his aunt and stepmother to his order, but later agreed on the basis that women are equal to men in their potential to achieve enlightenment. Buddha further removed all burdens from women. Women can be enlightened through their own efforts. Single women and widows were treated equally in Buddhism. As a result, many women escaped from the burden of households to join the order as fully ordained nuns. Monks and nuns in early Buddhism were treated equally by the Buddha.

However, only three months after the passing away of Buddha, the first Council was held. Five hundred enlightened monks were invited to it, and no nuns. Eight charges were laid against Ananda, the Buddha's cousin and attendant. One of them was that Ananda was responsible for having nuns included in the order.

Anyone reading the *Tripitaka* (the sacred book on doctrine and behaviour) without initiation can easily fall into the trap of thinking that Buddhism is biased against women and that Buddhism promotes patriarchy and is responsible for many social evils of which women have been victims. This would be a far cry from what was taught and practiced in the times of Lord Buddha. It is indeed sad that distorted interpretations gradually found their way into the teachings of the great Master. This is understandable, as in some Asian countries Buddhism has been the exclusive domain of monks. Buddhist women are expected to be traditionally conservative and submissive. Women are expected to participate only at the level of making offerings, and giving support to the temples and to the monks.[11] Similarly, diverse cultures construct their own version of what men and women are and ought to be.

Asian societies in general have been patriarchal and the scriptures of Asian religions have often been used to legitimize the male domination inherent in hierarchical power structures in society. Such twisted interpretations of religious teachings resulted in a distorted image of gender that lasted for many centuries. But in contrast, the Bible clearly states, ". . . So God created man in His own image, in the image of God He created them; male and female He created them" (Gen. 1:26-27). The text rescinds from creating the impression that the male is to dominate the female. This was not God's intention. The fall, however, introduces a separation and destroys the harmonious union, after which Adam began to blame Eve and God too. He said, "The woman whom thou gavest me, she gave me the fruit" (Gen. 3:12). Adam shirks his responsibility. God punished both man and woman but the woman is still directed towards man. God said, "Yet your desire shall be to your husband and he shall rule over you" (Gen. 3:16).

Thus, man who was created as a partner to woman now became her master. The rule of patriarchy was established. In the biblical tradition it appears as though the promise of God were fulfilled through the patriarchs. But this is only one side of the story. While patriarchy rightly focuses on three main actors – Abraham, Isaac and Jacob – it neglects the primary wife – Sarah, Rebecca and Rachel – who also figure prominently in the stories. In each case, it was these three who became the pivotal figures in the history of Israel. They became "vehicles" through whom God did "important things." Thus man and woman are ancestors and equal partners of faith. But this image has been distorted by introducing interpretations of patriarchy. The reasons for this can be many. Some are related to religious practices that belittle the status of women, unjust social structures that reduce and dehumanize her nature, and the fact that women strongly believe and accept their subservient role without raising any questions. Thus discrimination against women continues in terms of social status, economic situation, educational and academic achievements, cultural and political strength, etc.[12]

In Sri Lanka, it is not surprising that politics is a man's world. There are only around 14% women in politics, and that too because the majority of them were preceded by their fathers or husbands in politics. The fact that women hold up the country's economy (in the plantations, in the free-trade zones, and as domestic labour in the Middle East) is of little relevance in the area of decision making and influencing policy in the country.

Sex and Gender

While there are numerous studies on male/female stereotypes, social scientists are careful to distinguish between sex and gender. Sex sums up the biological dimorphic division of male and female, whereas gender refers to the social and cultural meaning attributed to biological differences.[13] As assessed by Craig, if gender is seen as being socially constructed, then the definitions of masculinity and femininity are the products of the interplay among a variety of social forces.

Gender can also be understood to vary spatially (from one culture to another) and temporarily (within any one culture over historical time). Different groups within any culture may also define masculinity and femininity differently, according to sub-cultural definitions, that is, race, ethnicity, age, class and the region of a country.[14]

Viewed from this perspective, it would be more appropriate to refer to gender in terms of "masculinity" and "femininity" than to be fixed on a single monolithic gender construct. In this context, there are some basic stereotype sex/gender behaviours that men and boys never recover from. A boy learns to perform years before he learns what the performing is for. Examples of boys climbing trees, scaling mountains, engaging in rough games, and being fed with better quality food (commonly found in Asia), mould the boy into the role model of the "tough guy" and the protector-breadwinner of the family already from his younger days.

Furthermore, even before the age of schooling, boys are prepared for the ritual of work. Well-intentioned, inquiring adults often want to know what boys would want to be when they grow up, meaning what profession, what occupation they would wish to pursue as adults. Thus boys, rather than girls, are seen as "doers." The games to which boys are introduced in the name of sports and physical education, such as football and basketball, are in fact simulated mini-battles to teach boys to compete in the game of life.

Difficulties Men Face

The reality, as summed up by Biddulph, is that men do not have a life of their own – they have just learned to pretend. This feeling of inadequacy has frequently manifested itself in the emotional behaviour of young men. As he grows into becoming a man, he realizes that there are huge energies that lay inside him and that are untapped. "He feels that there must be more, but does not know what that more is!"[15] He is unaware of the feminine forces within him, which can open new vistas in the pursuance of a meaningful life.

This "*being a male*" phenomenon has become more and more evident and compelling in Sri Lankan society. There are a number of young men, many of them university graduates, who consider themselves inadequate and misfits in society because they are without a job. A man without a job is made to feel inferior and worthless. Attempts are therefore being made to complement their education by offering various courses in management, accountancy, computer programming and the like at exorbitant costs so that they could match opportunities in the job market. The impression that the young man labours under is that what is lacking in him is a marketable storage of knowledge and skills to gain employment and to make him feel "manly." For the Asian man, employment is a vital component of his life as a man, for a woman it is seen as complementary to her domestic chores.

While the gender debate has raged for years, most participants have not woken up to the fact that "men are not winners." This may be of particular relevance to men in South Asia who are generally accepted to be the family's breadwinner. For example, very few men are happy (this is perhaps why in Sri Lanka the number of suicides are greater among men); and men and women are co-victims of a pattern of living that is in drastic need of revision.

Simply blaming men does not change anything! G. Corneau puts it succinctly: "The mass of men lead lives of quiet desperation."[16] Oppressive social, cultural and economic conditions have had their damaging effects on the physical and mental health of men. Kimbrell also attributes such conditions to the high rate of involvement of men in the criminal justice system. He notes the untreated post-war trauma in men, extensive unemployment and, for those with jobs, the experience of conflict between the demands of their job and the desire for time with their families.[17] Men are victims in a mechanized world where the human has little space to emerge. Kimbrell's reflections are based on statistics for the United States, but his inferences are valid for the Asian context as well.

Theological Androgyny and Its Problems

It had been proved beyond reasonable doubt that human beings are a complicated mix of masculine and feminine characteristics. Since purely "masculine" men and "feminine" women do not exist, the ideal to be pursued would be a balancing of both male and female psychological qualities where dominant masculinity and femininity are controlled. It is necessary that the gender equilibrium find expression in our institutions, laws, customs, and values if society is to experience a degree of sanity and conflicts are maintained at manageable levels. Perhaps the words of St. Paul, "There is no such thing as Jew or Greek, slave or free, male or female; you are all one person in Christ Jesus" (Gal. 3:28) could serve as a base for such ideological perception without obliterating the differences.

Theological androgyny intends to stress the humanity and equality of all people whatever be their sex, and to undermine ecclesiastical structures and social roles that tend to oppress socially insignificant men and women and deny them full human rights. "It promotes full ministerial equality between men and women, inclusive of liturgical language, sex neutral God-talk and the deconstruction of patriarchal authority."[18] Based on these premises it stands to reason to argue that religious institutions should accord full human rights and equal participation at every level of ministry and administration to both men and women. The argument gathers momentum and more weight when viewed in the context of fundamental human justice.

Simplistic notions that "*men are all alike*" or that "*women are basically the same*" are generalized stereotypes that tend to ignore the fact that human beings are a complex mixture of male and female, physical and spiritual, with emotional and psychic elements, and that male and female legal rights, career interests, social and family roles and religious sensibilities should not be regarded purely as a function of genitalia or in terms of gender. Post-modernization has contributed significantly to narrow such traditional and stereotype differences.

Any attempt, therefore, to deny equal treatment to males and females are generic "humans" with respect to legal rights and job opportunities, wage scales and position in ministry would be to distort what is obviously true. But, on the other hand, to believe that except for superficial genitalia there are no natural, emotional, distinctive psychological qualities between males and females that are complementary and can strengthen the liberation struggle of both oppressed men and women is to deny the instincts of the human heart. We must be ever so cautious of scientific investigation into gender differences that attempt to separate men and women to the extent of weakening the common bonds that bind them in their struggle to be human and against anti-democratic forces. This type of investigation will only contribute to gloss over the real issues of sexual exploitation that affect both men and women by engaging in a mere academic exercise on sexual differences.

On the other hand, repressing or obliterating sexual differences to produce the ideal androgynous person disguises a devastating attack on masculinity and males. One cannot forget that masculinity is founded on its distinctness from the feminine and energized by its continual contrast to femininity. All efforts to form the ideal androgynous creature bereft of sexual-emotional distinctiveness is an erroneous exercise. By suppressing male "excess" in aggression and competitiveness, and exaggerating "feminine" values such as harmony and relationship, one runs the risk of distorting and demasculinizing the male and denying him of his identity.

Revitalized Spirituality

Throughout her history, the Church contributed a fair share to the polarization of males and females, often becoming enmeshed in the prudery that was characteristic of the Victorian age.[19] There were missed opportunities where a greater focus on the positive qualities of the masculine and feminine could have strengthened the Church and her mission to promote stronger human bonds of friendship and mutual enrichment than be cast in the image of an invader.

The Church appears to have failed to provide meaning to many men. Male estrangement in spiritual matters is a well known though complicated phenomenon intertwined with psychological, social and religious factors. The Church as institution must share a part of the responsibility for this alienation of men from natural religiosity. The Church has not always understood men and spoken to them in a language they can comprehend and feel at home with.

Spirituality is not about some esoteric, mystic and unattainable object. Rather, it is the real concerns of men, which touch their deepest selves; their identity, their values, their relationships with their own selves, with others, and with God.

Dom Violi and Marie Joyce in a study in masculine identity

affirm that, "the movement of men toward spirituality is a revolutionary development overthrowing the legacy of several centuries of culturally indoctrinated hostility to spirituality begun by the Enlightenment, nurtured in the Industrial Revolution and brought to term by materialistic consumerism of today. These cultural movements have not *enthroned* man, as the critics of patriarchy would claim, rather, they have evicted men – out of the house, and out of themselves."[20]

Capitalism and consumerism have both shrunk men emotionally and weakened their spiritual capacity. In the West, they have become merely utilitarian, programmed to create capital. In the East, they are conditioned to serve the multinationals. Inevitably, these systems of bondage cannot satisfy man. Structural adjustment policies of the free market economy have further pauperized men – whether they be industrial workers or farmers. In the case of farmers in the Third World, subsidies have been reduced or removed reducing entire families to inhuman levels of poverty. This has only contributed to increasing the dependence of men on the unpaid labour of women and other members of the family. Men, therefore, yearn for something that would make them experience their inner force for freedom in a more tangible way. As a power force, this urge can, of course, be misdirected and can be used to fuel radical ideologies that end in political revolutions, or in fanatic religious fundamentalism.

The new men's spirituality is not another roadblock, says Dom Violi and Marie Joyce,[21] on the way to women's liberation – in some ways it is an outcome of it. The far reaching changes that feminism has created has made it necessary to demand a corresponding spirituality from men to free themselves from their own oppressiveness, numbness, and unconsciousness.

As mentioned earlier, men and women are biologically, psychologically and spiritually significantly different from one another. However, it cannot be denied that both men and women possess masculine and feminine characteristics, which they develop and express in different ways. Carl Jung employed *logos* and *eros* to explain distinct masculine and feminine features in persons. The ancient Chinese expressed this in terms of he *Yang* and the *Yin*. James M. Bowler, in his article "Transforming Iron John – Caring for the Male Soul," shows a preference for the terms *doing* (characterized by initiating, being self-reliant, assertive, controlling) in contrast to *being* (marked by being receptive, acquiescent, dependent, relational and vulnerable). These categories are, however, not exclusive and should never be used to fit men and women into well defined compartments. These characteristics must be viewed as complementary and not as mutually opposed and entirely contradictory. They are to be used in so far as they contribute to liberation from any form of bondage of both men and women.

With most men, it is important to use the *"doing"* as a point of entry to self-discovery, the affective, and the spiritual. Another way of expressing this is that men are much more comfortable talking about what they do for God, rather than how they are with God. When questioned, men are more likely to answer what they have done for Christ, what they are doing for Christ and what they should do for Christ. For women, the more appropriate questions they would prefer to answer are: how have I *been* with Christ? How *am* I with Christ? And how would I like *to be* with Christ?

Unlike women, men are more inclined to prioritize spirit and mind, and to view their bodies inferior to these. Differently from when they are in the sports field or in a health club – places of acute bodily consciousness – men find it difficult to make a connection with their bodies when they are in the context of prayer. Male spiritual consciousness is dualistic in the Platonic sense – outside of and above the body or nature. Thus, there is a tendency to equate holiness with bodilessness. For men, the unknown, mysterious transcendent God is beyond – external to their self. God is *"up there"* rather than deep within. James Nelson maintains that this dualism is due to biological differences or the genitalization of sexuality,[22] though one fails to understand how genitalia alone could explain this Cartesian duality. Could the concept of "gender" be helpful to lead us out of this labyrinthian duality, or is the duality a normative feature to be pursued at all costs? Most emphatically 'no'!

For men, says Nelson, external sex organs communicate that the unknown mystery is out there. Male sex is giving rather than receiving and is associated with a certain performance anxiety. But one wonders how Nelson fails to see that the male sex not merely gives, but is also prone to take whatever is precious to the female whenever the opportunity presents itself! Human history and the history of invasions of the weak by the strong will easily bear this out.

Nelson's *separation phenomenon* also dissociates sex from the self and, otherwise than for women, from intimacy. For most women sexuality is internal, immanent and mysterious, while for most men it is external and instrumental. The danger that one sees in this dualistic approach is the failure to observe the complementarity of the sexes which is more vital to construct a harmonious human being where both the masculine and the feminine meet and interact.

It also needs to be emphasized here that since not many men are yet ready to deal with a feminine image of God, one must be aware of the tendency in men to project their father relationship on to their operating image of God.

Challenge for the Church

The paradoxical fact is that while the Church's political structure is clearly patriarchal and male-dominated, its spirituality is directed heavily towards females and is quite alienating to men. There is a sub-conscious feeling among many men that Christian spirituality requires a kind of emancipation – that it is something reserved for the odd, the old, the sick, the asexual, or those "out of gas." Often men prefer to keep their distance from the Church, to remain in the periphery of involvement, in the back of the Church, or they simply decide to go their own way.

Men who are active in the profane world of business and politics relate to the world of prayer and worship by proxy, that is, by the saving feminine presence in their lives (wife, mother, daughter), or through an occasional contact with a spiritual man, a priest, a monk and an occasional visit to a church or shrine. This is the outcome of Christian Platonism, viz., that women are *naturally* religious while men are carnal, interested only in the material world and its benefits.

Dom Violi and Marie Joyce have pointed out that "applying the gospel lesson to the male-female antagonism, we have to conclude that men, the supposedly dominant group, are in great or greater need of salvation when compared to women. They think they have power, but they are mostly powerless. They think they have freedom, but they are largely unliberated. They think they are lords, defining reality, but in fact they are trapped – trapped by success and performance."

If we are to go by the gospel, then the fulfillment of humanity will not be found in domination, but in service and partnership; not in power wielding but in power sharing. The implications of partnership and sharing are that human beings have been called to live in community, in co-operation, in solidarity and communion between otherwise opposed social groups. Today we speak of resource sharing between the First and the Third Worlds, between the developed and developing countries, power sharing between majority and minority ethnic groups. These implications for the community are analogously valid for personal spirituality as well as viewed in the context of gender.

Conclusion

There is little doubt that men have held the predominance of power for the past two centuries. Therefore, it is inevitable that male dominance be referred to when studying recent gender history. It has been said that men often acted thoughtlessly, sometimes viciously and nearly always for their own advantage when dealing with women as sex. Viewed from this perspective, men would surface as faceless oppressors. Such a simplistic approach to male gender through generalizations cannot do justice to the varieties of male behaviour or the complexities of inner motives. Besides, this does not help us to understand how gender operates as a cultural and political force, nor how to negotiate a viable future where masculine and feminine qualities combine to inspire and sustain a better world for all.

Jorgen Moltmann and Elisabeth Moltmann-Wendel, in their recent book, *God – His and Hers*, share their insights that the recognition of the difference between the sexes is grounded less in biology than in social experience, so that in looking to Christian faith and practice in the future, it is important to begin from the historical experience of women and men as they can be discovered from social psychology and personal testimony. Here we find an orientation for gender studies in the future, not merely to understand the differences between masculine and feminine, but also the complementary factors that could contribute to constructing a new gender paradigm.

Notes

1. See Craig, S., (ed.) *Men, Masculinity and the Media*, Newbury Park: Sage, 1992; Farrell, W., *The Liberated Man*, New York, 1975; Lawlor, R., *Earth Honouring: The New Male Sexuality*, Newtown, Australia, 1989; Pfeil, F., *White Guys*, London, 1995; Williams, B., and Gardener, G., *Men, Sex, Power and Survival*, Elwood, Greenhouse, 1989.

2. Pfeil, F., *White Guys, op. cit.*, p. xiii.

3. In Sri Lanka, even though the current war that has lasted for 18 years is presently being waged by the dictates of a woman President who was ushered into power on the popularity of her slain husband, there is a subtle feeling lurking in the minds of many that as a woman she does not fit into the stereotype of a warmonger. Many thought of her as the standard-bearer of peace and her role model was

expected to be that of a 'peace maker.' Posters depicted her in this role model with doves and holding the hands of children to drive home this image.

4. See Greer, G., *The Female Eunuch*, London, Granada, 1971; Jaegar and Struhl, P., *Feminist Frameworks*, New York, 1978; Saunders and Evans (eds.)., *Gender Relations in Australia*, 1983; Williams and Garnener, *Men, Sex, Power and Survival*.

5. See O'Connor, P., *The Inner Man*, Melbourne, 1993; Phillips, *The Trouble with Boys*, London, 1994; Rotundo, E.A., *American Manhood*, New York, 1993.

6. Filene, P., *Man in the Middle*, New Jersey, 1981, p. 90.

7. Biddulph, S., *Manhood*, Sydney, 1984.

8. Craig, S., *Men, Masculinity and the Media, op. cit.*

9. Rousseau, J.J., *The First and Second Discourses*, New York, 1964, p. 166.

10. Thirucharidran, Selvy, *The Politics of Gender and Women's Agency in Post Colonial Sri Lanka*, 1997, p. 1-4.

11. Kabilsingh, C., *Feminist Buddhist Discourses*, Concilium, 1996/1, p. 62-65.

12. Peter, Navamani, "Biblical Paradigms for Women's Ministry in Asia," *Theology for Our Times*, No. 5, June 1998, Indian School of Ecumenical Theology, pp. 99-101.

13. Hamachek, D., *Encounters with the Self*, New York, 1978.

14. See Craig, *Men, Masculinity and the Media*, op. cit., Shelton, B.A., and John, D., "Ethnicity, Race and Difference: A Comparison of White, Black and Hispanic Men's Households," in Hood (ed.), *Men, Work and Family*.

15. Biddulpl, S., *Manhood, op.cit.*, p. 2.

16. Corneau, G., *Absent Farmers – Lost Sons*, Boston, 1991; Farrell, W., *The Why Men Are The Way They Are*, Filene, P., *Men in the Middle, op.cit.*, Farmer, S., *The Wounded Male*, New York, 1991.

17. Kimbrell, A., *The Masculine Mystique: The Politics of Masculinity*, New York, 1995.

18. Dom Violi and Joyce, M., *Searching for Masculine Identity*, p. 360.

19. See Foucault, Michel, *The History of Sexuality*, in Continental Philosophy, Blackwell, USA, 1998, p. 381.

20. Dom Violi and Joyce M., *Searching for Masculine Identity*, p. 358.

21. Dom Violi and Joyce M., *Searching for Masculine Identity*, p. 358.

22. Nelson, James B., *The Intimate Connection: Male Sexuality and Masculine Spirituality*, Philadelphia, 1988, p. 29-46.

Gender Concern
A Male Perspective in Wholistic Paradigm

J.B. Banawirmata

On the cross, Jesus symbolizes the exact opposite of male dominating power. Rather, on the cross, power is poured out in self-sacrificing love. The cross is *kenosis* of patriarchy. Looking at the cross, some feminists have reflected that sociologically it was probably better that the incarnation happened in a male human being; for if a woman had preached and enacted compassion and given the gift of self even unto death, the world would have shrugged – is not this what women are supposed to do anyway? But for a man to live and die this way in a world of male privilege is to challenge the patriarchal ideal of the dominating male at its root. (Johnson, 1990:111).

A Male Experience in Indonesian Context

Sociologically speaking it might be true that male feminists have certain advantages in promoting gender justice. Once I was invited by an Islamic woman from a state public office to talk with provincial government officials about equal partnership between men and women. I told her to invite a more appropriate speaker, namely a woman. Her response was exactly the opposite. It is better to have a man, especially a priest, talking about this theme (even if the audience was religiously mixed). If a woman speaks about equal partnership, men will think that it is only a matter of self-defense and not a fundamental claim of being human. This is underlining of course the fact that cultural settings give privilege to men and priests whereas women are humiliated. On many occasions, among Christians or inter-religious groups, I never experienced their rejection of my message of feminist thoughts. At most, there has been misunderstanding and hesitancy.

Indonesian Bishops' Conferences positively evaluate women's movements in Indonesia. The Pastoral Letter of Easter 1999 (*Arise and Be Unwavering in Hope*) mentioned some signs of hope. "There is concern for the fate of others, particularly those who are neglected, poor and weak, including the defense of children's and women's rights." "The women's movement has always been a quiet strength that has an extensive impact, exhibits love and sensitivity that touches and concurrently gives genuine vitality to the nation's struggle for life." The pastoral letter did not speak about a women's movement within the (Roman Catholic) Church, but within the society as a whole. It seems it is true that the inter-faith women's movement in the society is much more outspoken and visible than within the Roman Catholic Church. It is a positive sign, but also a negative one corresponding to the lack of development within the Roman Catholic Church.

The participation and activity of women within the Protestant churches seem to be stronger, not only by the fact that there are already many women ministers but also there is already an Association of Women Theologians (*PERWATI = Persekutuan Wanita Berpendidikan Teologi di Indonesia*). At the beginning of the year 2000, this Association published *Sophia*, a Journal of Theologizing of Women in Indonesia. The comparison between Catholics and Protestants falls back partly on their different structures.

Women's movements in Indonesia have brought together people of different faiths for human concerns. On certain occasions Moslem women have taken leading initiatives. In the meantime inter-faith women's movements are focusing on protesting violence against women and advocacy for women victims. The suffering women and the victims pull together all feminist groups. I have never seen a women's NGO co-opted by the power structure. The problems seem to be conflicts between individuals that sometimes result in serious difficulties, since that which is personal is also political.

However, at the same time, there are women who resist efforts to improve women's conditions. On several occasions I have heard women saying: "Women are comfortable with their position, they feel at home and enjoy living in a patriarchal world. Instead of claiming for their rights, they prefer the status quo, why should we change?" This attitude has a *self-centered approach* to social change, and perceives transformation from an individual concern only. The internalization of patriarchy among women is surely supported by the actual culture and structure of the society.

There are also other approaches to change, namely, an *outward looking approach*. With this perspective, women involve themselves in female gender concerns for emancipation not for an individual alone, but for the betterment of all. This kind of outlook might be more appealing to those who hesitate to join the movement. Besides that, feminist movements as counter cultures and counter structures need to find a paradigm and discourse that are more appropriate, that also offer more fundamental orientations to life's complexities. This small paper will suggest a wholistic paradigm approach.

Feminism in Wholistic Paradigm

Diarmuid O'Morschu differentiates between a wholistic system and a mechanistic system as follows (1997:25):

Mechanistic	Wholistic
1. The whole equals the sum of the parts.	1. The whole is greater than the sum of the parts.

2. Every system or structure consists of isolated, unrelated, autonomous parts.	2. Everything consists of parts continually inter-, relating a process characterized by interdependence and mutual cooperation.
3. Basic metaphor is the machine.	3. Basic metaphor is the *holon* (the whole).
4. Change or repair demands mechanical interference and manipulation.	4. All life forms have an innate self-organization potential which is undermined by mechanical interference.
5. Every aspect is studied through observation, quantification, dissection and manipulation.	5. Since the whole is greater than the sum of the parts, our understanding is always partial and must remain open to new and fuller understanding.
6. Modification and change are effected from outside.	6. Change and healing are effected from within, possibly by a change-agent acting from without.
7. We can control the machine, and therefore, we model everything on mechanical processes.	7. We don't need to control; trust the unfolding process.
8. Objectivity and emotional non-involvement are the basic virtues.	8. Participation and feeling for the whole are the basic virtues.

In a general description, a comparison between the wholistic or cosmic paradigm and the mechanistic or secularist paradigm description does not aim to uncover their details and existing variants. However, they can challenge us to be aware of the paradigm we use and its implications in communicating our gender concerns.

The mechanistic paradigm perceives reality as *instrumental*. Here the cosmic is separated from the meta-cosmic, and therefore tends to desacralize the cosmic universe. The result of the Enlightenment process is that nature and society are demythologized, meaning that both nature and society are not any longer considered static and magic but as objects which can be examined and enhanced by human beings. This view, on the other hand, has produced the *technological age*, where we witness the development of science and technology and their applications in modern industry and economy. And this perspective is seen as bringing about success and prosperity as the sources of satisfaction and happiness. On the other hand, this pattern *aggressively* conquers nature and enhances an attitude to exploit nature as a mere object and to destroy the human environment. The cosmic universe is desacralized.

In contrast, the cosmic paradigm perceives reality as *sacramental*, the cosmic is related to and symbolizes the meta-cosmic. The meta-cosmic manifests itself in the cosmic. Here the religious aspect is included. The eight characteristics of the wholistic paradigm mentioned above are values to struggle for through the movement of liberation in all dimensions of life.

Nevertheless, it is important to be aware of the weakness of the wholistic paradigm, namely, being manipulated by negative forces of the *status quo*. Sometimes the meta-cosmic is used as an argument in such a way that the cosmic is not seriously taken into account. Negative forces will stand against *critical emancipation*, against *the dynamic and social change* needed for the better of the whole.

The Javanese worldview for example perceives the *universal cosmos with a harmonious hierarchical and collective order*. The cosmos includes the visible world and the invisible world, nature and society, both internal and external shapes. All have certain and appropriate places. Therefore, the society is ordered hierarchically and collectively and the stratification is harmonious. There is a hierarchy of the powerful (*wong gedhe*) and there is also a collective life of the powerless (*wong cilik*). The Javanese identity and personality are manifested in the internal sensitivity (*rasa*) which feels the cosmic and social structure in order to identify one's right place and role and to adapt oneself with the existing harmony. This refined attitude (*halus*) will bring about spiritual happiness and peace. On the other hand, a rude attitude (*kasar*) which puts too much emphasis on the material world and oneself, disturbs the harmony and will eventually be in vain and lead to failure. This religious-social ethos is *wisdom moral* in accordance with an individual person's place and role. The harmony principle avoids conflicts, and the principle of respect toward superiors supports hierarchical social patterns. They can help regulate and solidify the society but they can also promote the attitude of waiting for a superior's order or loyalty that enhances an authoritarian political system.

However, in the Javanese culture, there are also many practices promoting the wholistic paradigm in the positive sense. It appears in the practice of *musyawarah* (communal consultation and consensus), *gotong-royong* (communal work and help), *kerja bakti* (communal work and service) that are usually integrated with religious rituals (cf. Banawiratma and Mueller 1999:152-155). The wholistic paradigm perceives the self interrelated with neighbours and nature as well as with gods and God.

GOD

———

SELF

NEIGHBOURS ——— NATURE
(Men and Women)

———

GOODS

Human beings, man and woman, as the image of God, are understood as a collective personality who are, together with God, co-responsible for the whole creation. Human justice becomes one with eco-justice. What is liberative for women neighbours is also liberative for men neighbours, for self, nature and goods in God. Accordingly, A. Pieris speaks about "human liberation as a cosmic experience of the meta-cosmic. The experience of the meta-cosmic is not liberation from the cosmic, but liberation from secularism. The cosmic dimension is never lost in human liberation" (1996:61).

If certain dimensions of the basic relationships are cut off, the negative aspect of other relationships will suddenly become very prominent. Therefore, in a society, which respects spiritual values, very strong materialism is often observed. In an all-secular society, we might find a false religion or a religious sect which only exploits human beings.

The liberation of women and the rediscovery of the feminine in the cosmic wholistic paradigm are involving new ways of *relating to life* that include participation of all people. The powerless are called to liberation and self-empowerment. "Power is called to be accountable; power is challenged to share, to care, to cherish, and, above all, to let go of its monopoly of interference and domination" (O'Murchu, 1997:155). It is true not only within the secular world but also within our churches.

In his reflection on the cosmic and feminist component, A. Pieris concludes the following nine important statements (1996:61-62):

1. The cosmic approach is sacramental; it sees and says more than the secularist perspective, which, being reductionist, stops at what the senses perceive. If the instrumental approach to the world is a product of secularism, the feminist approach is cosmic by nature.

2. Self-love and self-affirmation point to a mere remedial measure to cure the effects of instrumentalization of women; but it is not a preventive measure unless we abandon the secularist

model with its liberal philosophy of self-indulgence and individualism which has accelerated the current gyne-ecological crisis.

3. The cosmic is dialectical, with male and female forces (gnosis and agape) interacting in its journey toward self-transcendence. This is not an undue "generalization" but a description of the subliminal instincts of the human psyche which continue their dialectics with the predominance of one or the other of them whatever be the sexual orientation of a person, be it homo– or hetero-. Hence, the next observation.

4. The secularist view being what it is – a perception of a desacralized, mechanized and masculinized world – does not maintain the tension between male gnosis and female agape, which is an indispensable element of the movement for liberation; but the cosmic, by maintaining this biopolarity, prevents masculinization.

5. Consequently, a cosmic spirituality preserves the womanly, the earthly and the bodily contribution to the salvific experience.

6. The cosmic implies religiousness, which is associated with openness to the meta-cosmic or the humanum; the secularist approach is a sealing of the world against its own transcendent destiny. Thus a cosmic worldview is also human centered.

7. Feminism, therefore, is a permanent feature in the struggle for full humanity in that it maintains the cosmic dimension without which the experience of the meta-cosmic (i.e., absolute liberation) is impossible.

8. Hence all religious systems that overemphasize the meta-cosmic pursuits at the risk of ignoring the cosmic roots of religious experience tend to be patriarchal; feminism is, therefore, the name for the endless struggle to retain the cosmic religiosity alive within these major religions.

9. All this means that feminism also serves as a permanent critique of religion. Religion cannot survive in the future without appropriating the feminist critique, just as feminism cannot achieve its liberative goal without the aid of a religion so critiqued.

One might ask why did Pieris keep the words "female" and "male" in his formulation no. 4: "the tension between *male gnosis* and *female agape*, which is an indispensable element of the movement for liberation." Is it not better to erase these words, since all that are mutually exchanged between male and female belong to a culturally constructed gender relationship? However, in formulation no. 3, it is clear that Pieris does not want to maintain an undue "genderization." The point of cosmic feminism is to maintain the tension and the dynamic toward the final liberative goal.

Participation of All for All

Participation and feeling for the whole are the basic virtues in a wholistic paradigm. The participation of all is very valuable for the whole. The responsibility for participation implies the demand "Don't take away my participation." The participation of women is not just the demand of women's dignity and women's right, it is very important for men, for the community, for all. All participants are not only inward looking or ego-oriented, but outward moving to the whole.

In a wholistic paradigm, *the priority of the victims*, the oppressed, the suffering and the marginalized becomes a priority for the betterment of the whole. They are the vicars of Christ in this world, with whom we are called to act for and to be with (cf. Matt. 25:31-46). They are the ones to whom the movement of God's Reign is entrusted. Our liberative struggle is participating in God's liberative force. To overcome victimization; one cannot avoid conflict with victimizers that embody the power of the Anti-God. This is the experience of the prophets that stand on the side of God with the victims.

The Spirit that we call the Spirit of Christ is the same Spirit of God that is present in human beings and in the world. Following Iraeneus, we can describe God working with two hands, with the Word and the Spirit. The word becoming a human being in Jesus 2000 years ago does not stop God from speaking to the world today. The same Spirit of God and of Jesus is moving in the world now. We are called to find the presence and action of the Spirit everywhere. In the wholistic paradigm, the gender concern is interrelated to inter-faith, inter-cultural and inter-racial dialogue. The same Spirit relates all to all.

Within our Christian faith we say that we have to accept all given charisma for the serving of community. To suppress certain charisma in women or others means to suffer losses. The way to live openly leads to a communal discernment, decision and action. While trusting the unfolding process, the liberation of women and the rediscovery of the feminine in a wholistic paradigm becomes a counter and alternative culture, a new vision and a new way to relate to life.

References

Banawiratma, J.B. dan Muller, J., 1999, *Contextual Social Theology: An Indonesian Model*, EAPR, Vol. 36, No. 1-2, Manila: EAPI.

Johnson, Elizabeth A., 1990, *Consider Jesus: Waves of Renewal in Christology*, New York: Crossroad.

O'Murchu, Diarmiud, 1997, *Our World in Transition, Making Sense of a Changing World*, Sussex, The Book Guild Ltd.

Pieris, Aloysius, 1996, *Fire and Water*, Maryknoll, New York: Orbis Books.

Sophia, Jurnal Berteologi Perempuan Indonesia, Vol. 1, No. 1, Maret 2000, Jakarta: Persekutuan Wanita Berpendidikan Teologi di Indonesia.

The Portrait of Women in the Parables

Kemdirim O. Protus

Introduction

"Jesus was a feminist"[1] is the title of a work by Leonard Swindler. If by feminism we understand a new world, a new way of seeing and acting, a critique of cultural assumptions in relation to gender, new possibilities of justice in society, inclusiveness[2] and practice of tenderness, then the liberating message of Jesus as recorded in the gospels immensely points to Jesus as being on the side of woman. Apparently, the gospel accounts are replete with references to those women who ministered to Jesus, who were delegated to announce the "good news" and who gave silent witness to immense agonies.

The purpose of this paper is to delineate the image of women in Jesus' parables. The paper makes the point that while it is true that New Testament parables are dominated by men and male activities, women are also models for the true character of God. Like men, their actions in the parables portray what the reign of God means.

We shall first offer a brief definition of the term parable, then outline and discuss the specifically women-oriented parables, and finally its implications both for woman and the African church.

The Term "Parable" Defined

The English word "Parable" is from the Greek *parabole* which means placing things side by side for comparison.[3] Its Hebrew equivalent *mashal* or figurative form of expression refers to a variety of non-literal material in the Old Testament.[4] Also, the German word for parable, *Gleichness*, if translated, means likeness. Thus, a parable can be described as a narrative in which image and reality are compared even fictitiously. It can also be true to life. Indeed as C.H. Dodd[5] observes, in a parable truth is expressed through concrete pictures rather than abstraction. One peculiar thing about a parable is that it is a story with a particular religious or ethical purpose. It is always thought provoking and often a challenge to decisive action.

In the Old Testament, the use of parables reflects an ancient, culturally universal method of teaching an ethical lesson applicable to everyday life, by using symbolic stories with concrete characters and actions.[6] Here, parables refer to open-ended metaphors, allegorical parallels to historical events, or short stories about God's covenantal fidelity and the community's way of being God-like in the world. It is in Ezekiel that we largely find the use of parabolic language. Take for example, the use of metaphors of the burned wood of the useless grape vine (Ezek. 15:1-8), and the uprooted vine which is replanted in dry desert (Ezek. 19:10-14). These describe the sad fortunes of exiled Israel, once God's chosen vine. Other parabolic discourses and images that either instruct and console the community (Jer. 18:1-6, 24:1-20; Ezek. 34:1-31, 37:1-14; Hos. 3:1-5, 2:1-3) or communicate restoration after the exile (Isa. 35:1-10, 65:10-11, 66:7-16; Ezk. 40:1-48) certainly abound. Though the extent to which parables are understood by the community is not known, one thing is however clear. They confront a community with a different picture of God or a more inclusive social vision (gender perspective) than ones they have cherished.

In the New Testament, parables refer to Jesus' teaching stories, often about the reign of God. It covers such forms as proverbs (Luke 4:23), maxims (Luke 14:7-11), riddles (Mark 7:15-17), examples (Luke 12:15-21), figurative speech (Mark 4:33), similes (Matt. 13:33), metaphors (Matt. 5:14), and parables themselves. Current theoretical analysis of New Testament parables suggest that although they are often written as similes (e.g., one thing compared to another, such as disciples sent out "as lambs in the midst of wolves" – Luke 10:3), they function more like metaphors, in which a feature or quality of one thing is directly attributed to another (e.g., "You are the salt of the earth" – Matt. 5:13)[7]. It is in this understanding that parable includes the above mentioned figurative expressions. Like the Old Testament, Jesus' parables in the New Testament are drawn from everyday life (Luke 11:5-8) and as such they have a sense of real life experience about them. They are full of paradoxes (Luke 14:21ff) and challenges (e.g., Mark 4:9, Matt. 20:15, 21-31, 13:45-46). The real novelty in New Testament parables is the use of women as true models exhibiting the character of God.

Women-Centred Parables

Parables occupy a substantial part of the teaching method adopted by Jesus. Most of his insightful teachings about the Kingdom of God were done in parabolic expression. While some of these parables are designed to appeal primarily to men, others are focused on women. Among such are The Lost Sheep and The Lost Coin, The Mustard Seed and The Leaven, and The Bridegroom's Attendants and The Bride's Attendants. Others include the saying concerning The Men in the Field and The Women at the Mill (Matt. 24:40 ff) as well as The Patch and the Wineskins (Matt. 9:16ff; Mark 2:21ff; Luke 5:36-39ff) and, perhaps The Moth and The Rust (Matt. 6:19ff; Luke 12:33).

Specifically, however, four of these parables have women as their chief character. These parables bring to focus women's perspectives in Jesus' teaching. They are:

1. The Parable of the Leaven (Matt. 15:33; Luke 13:20-21)
2. The Lost Coin (Luke 15:8-10)
3. The Persistent Widow (Lk. 18:1-8)
4. The Ten Virgins (Matt. 25:1-13)

1. The Parable of the Leaven (Matt. 13:33; Luke 13:20-21)

The Parable of the Leaven ranks with the parable of the mustard seed in what Joachim Jeremiah[8] refers to as paired or double parables. These parables are paired in Matthew and Luke (e.g., one about a man, the other about a woman) reflecting beautifully the evenhanded fairness of Jesus to both sexes. The parable of the Leaven is found in Q (par Luke 13:20-21). In its present form it falls into the same pattern with the parables of the sower and the mustard seed, illustrating the irresistible growth of the reign of the kingdom from small beginnings.

The parable is set in the domestic world of women's culinary activities. To be remembered is that, in Jewish tradition, it was the privilege of the chief woman of the household to knead the bread for the entire family. It is no wonder the reign of God's kingdom is compared to the yeast a woman puts in the dough she is making. But the kingdom of heaven is not "like leaven," rather it is like the prepared, risen dough[9] (cf. Rom. 11:16) thus underscoring as it were the action of the woman in the enterprise. Clearly as it should be understood, the yeast a woman kneads into dough makes everyone in the community, as it were, rise and be capable of satisfying the hunger of others.[10] This would mean that women are also subjects in the household of God.

Though leaven in Jewish tradition often had the symbolic meaning of evil, exceptions can be found.[11] It is even more significant that in Syria, till today, leaven is held "in high and reverential esteem." In fact, it represents fertility. Accordingly, it is customary to paste a lump of leavened dough on the lintel of the door by which a bride enters her new home. As she enters her friends would say: "May you be as blessed and fruitful as the *Khamera*.[12] However the leaven is taken, it is characteristic of Jesus' parables to contain surprising features.

Indeed, while in the version of the mustard seed the chief character is a man, in the leaven story it is a woman. It follows well that the action of both man and woman qualifies as analogies for the reign of God. The parable is a pointer to the fact that while women's area of activity especially in Africa is largely domestic, their action, though lowly are no less salvific.

2. The Lost Coin (Luke 15:8-10)

This parable is without parallel in other gospels. In other words, it is peculiar to Luke. On the other hand, in the overall consideration of the parables, it is associated with the Lost Sheep (Matt. 18:12) and the Prodigal Son, also peculiar to Luke. The principal figure in the Lost Coin parable is a common woman from among the people. The parable known for its brevity, clarity and compassion tells the effort of the woman to search for her lost coin and the hearty joy she exudes at finding it. This is compared to the joy of the heavenly host over the repentance of a sinner.

Ordinarily, a woman losing her coin is nothing new in an ordinary village set up. What is astonishing, however, is her action. In the great search for the lost coin, the poor woman exerted much energy. For her no difficulty is too great; perhaps she even wounds herself in the heat of her search, more so as everything has to be swept, turned upside down, packed and unpacked. The woman demonstrates the personal determination inherent in women to succeed in life.

The desperate and worrisome manner in which the poor woman in this parable sought for her lost coin cast some light on the social conditions of the other women mentioned elsewhere in the scriptures: the poor widow who put in two small coins in the treasury (Luke 21:1-4), and also the poor widow whose only son was raised to life (Luke 7:11-17). Being part of the group in Jewish tradition that is known as the *anawim* – the poor ones of Yahweh[13] the widow's plight is very precarious, always at the threshold of penury. It is no wonder that Jesus praised the heroism of the widow's sacrificial offer of the only coin she had to live on.

It is typical of Luke to bring women into the picture of Jesus' ministry. This is not without reason. Indeed, for Luke and Jesus, women are agents of evangelization. It follows that the full meaning of the parable is revealed in the events that precede the narrative. Jesus is in the company of sinners and the indignation of the Jewish religious leaders. The fact, as Pol Vonck[14] rightly observes, is that through the Lucan life-setting, the parable of the lost coin acquires a polemical character. Jesus now uses it, as it were, the story of a woman in search of her lost coin, to rebuke the Pharisees' and Scribes' aloofness and avoidance of "tax-collectors and sinners." This parable as Vonck says is part of Jesus' answer to their grumblings.[15]

In the parable, however, Luke underscores the potentialities in women. While in the previous parable it is patience, in this one it is faith and determination. Indeed, like the searching shepherd, the woman, as a figure for God, searches with determination for the one missing coin needed to complete the monetary unit of ten pieces, much like a deck of cards that is useless if one is missing.

3. The Persistent Widow (Luke 18:1-8)

This is another parable that is found only in Luke. It is almost a doublet of the parable of a friend at Midnight (Luke 11:5-8). It narrates a sorry story of a poor widow who presents a case against an adversary[16] before an unjust judge. The judge proved hard and unmoved but capitulates because he is besieged to the limits of endurance. The widow batters down the door of his resistance. As earlier observed, throughout the Bible, the widow is the type and representative of those in need of compassion and practical help (Exod. 22:22; Deut. 10:18; Jer. 22:3; Isa. 1:17, 23). They might be quite young but their status in society was very low. They suffered insecurity and were subject to contempt and injustice.

The parable presents us with difficulties. First, who is the chief character in the parable, the judge or the widow? Second, is the stress to be laid on the petitioning or the granting of the plea? More than this, besides the widow, three principal characters appear before us namely: her adversary, the judge and God. Concerning the principal character, though commentators are not agreed as to whether the widow or the judge is the important character, it is obvious that by his editorial introduction (v.1) Luke shifts attention away from the judge to the woman, thus making her the example of persistent prayer.[17] On the other hand, too, Jesus' question at the end, however, makes it clear that the judge is meant to be the central figure.[18] Nonetheless, it is remarkable that the point of the story is the responsiveness of God to those who cry unto Him. It is such then that the widow represents the groups in the society who are excluded, alienated, discriminated against, that is to say, all who suffer injustice and are kept poor thereby.

Further, as William Barclay[19] suggests, the judge is not of Jewish stock but is likely one of the Roman magistrates, appointed by Herod, who were notorious for taking brides. The widow, on the other hand, stands for the poor, oppressed and defenseless people in the society. In fact, in the parable God is not likened to the wicked judge but is rather contrasted to him. Hence, the remark, "You see what that wicked judge did, will God not show justice to his elect [and in our context represented by the woman] who call upon him day and night even when he delays" (vv. 6-7).

Luke, again in this classic parable, demonstrates the qualities endowed in women. Determination and persistence, steadfastness and confidence, etc., are the lots of women. Luke draws out the lesson that God will not abandon his people if only they remain faithful and steadfast in prayer (like the woman) until Jesus comes. Further, Luke uses the image of a woman to show how God is disposed to listen to the cry of the poor with unwearied patience. Indeed, the parable is a story of courage and audacity in the face of obstacles which women too represent. The widow in the parable is a shining example to African widows who must be bold and courageous in the demand for their rights even in the face of difficult social structures.

4. The Ten Virgins (Matt. 25:1-13)

This is another twin parable, giving the feminine counterpart to 24:45-51 – the parable of the servant entrusted with supervision. It is peculiar to Matthew and the story is one of the seven so-called *parousia* parables in the gospel of Matthew. Like the other six, it contains three themes: that the Messiah is coming for Judgement Day, that the time of His arrival is unforeseeable, and that there is need for preparation.[20] Thus, the parable calls for readiness and preparedness for the reception of the kingdom of God when it dawns and also warns against unpreparedness, carelessness and superficiality in the Christian life.

The parable, however, presents a lot of problems for its fuller interpretation and understanding. It is often argued whether the parable came from Jesus or is a creation of the early church. It is even difficult to imagine why the bride is never mentioned. This is not all. Reginald Fuller[21] opines that the parable contains several puzzling details – whose house was the groom entering, the bride's or his own, and in whose house did the marriage feast take place? What made the groom arrive late? Would a wedding feast have taken place after midnight? As a matter of fact, the precise matrimonial situation is impossible to reconstruct.

But it is rather clear that women dominate the characters in the parable. A woman's world of ten lamp-carrying virgins is here offered as metaphorical parallel to the story of the three male servants given talents (Matt. 25:14-30). Like the third servant who buries his money, five of the women prove to be foolish and unprepared for delay. The parable describes how to live wisely and self-responsively in the world. Awaiting the arrival of the last day is imaged by the opening of the door to the wedding banquet, bringing joy to those women who endured to the end.

The principal lesson is the importance of preparedness and of single-mindedness in view of the challenge of the hour. It goes well that the parable echoes the positive and negative qualities in women. The improvident girls were not merely forgetful but were culpably careless and as a result they forfeited the opportunity to "enter into the joy" which ought to be theirs. Their failure to be present at the decisive moment points to the fickle mindedness in women. The responses of the wise virgins are also noteworthy. It is the attitude of women that half measure cannot work, especially when available time is limited. The fact is that, like men, women too realize that our relationship to God is something to be recognized and lived out during one's life time. It is not something to be borrowed at the eleventh hour.

Implication for Women and the Church

The four parables in the synoptic gospels with bearing on women's activities have tremendous implications both for woman and the African church. In the first place, as I observed elsewhere,[22] in his ministry, Jesus shows that his liberating power is for men and women who especially are economically, physically, socially, and culturally unfortunate. In these situations of deprivation, however, women are most disadvantaged. To accentuate the equality of the sexes and thus restore the dignity of womanhood battered and morally wounded by the Jewish culture of his era, Jesus radically used women as major characters in his parables. This no doubt puts him an age above his contemporary Jewish rabbis who found it rather difficult to use images of women to depict God or to express the people's religiosity. It was a novel revolutionary act intended as it were to reduce the incidence of discrimination against women in Jewish public life. In recognizing the action of the lowly and less regarded people in the society – women – as model actions depicting the expectation of candidates for heaven, Jesus raises them not only as people but characters to be emulated.

In these parables, Jesus attempts to convey the feminine or motherly image of God (love, care, justice, affection, friendliness, sympathy and warmth) and the basic qualities inherent in women (tenacity, determination, patience, conviction, and generosity, etc.) necessary for the proclamation of the good news. Take for example, the parable of the leaven (Matt. 13:33) (e.g., where the woman mixes yeast with flour). The flour's rising and filling the whole place is a classic example of what love more than abundance can do to provide for everyone. Also in the action of the woman in the parable of the lost coin (Luke 15:8-9), the evangelist demonstrates the absolute love and forgiveness of God as a loving father and mother who is always searching for the lost member of the family. It is indeed fascinating that women in the parables are used to depict the true character of God. Thus, Jesus depicts God's true character of supreme mystery that can neither be predicted nor taken for granted in the parable of the Ten Virgins (Matt. 25:1-13).

The parables of the leaven, the lost coin, the unjust judge, the widow and the ten virgins, can easily be set in the scenes of African cultural life. It is no gain-saying that the laborious search of the woman who lost her coin or the one that prepares the dough parallel the resourcefulness of the African woman who toils day and night for the well-being of the household. The fearless posture of the widow in the face of the wicked judge is no less akin to the assertiveness of the African widow bringing up her children in the face of hunger and hardship. Of course, the lesson drawn from this enables African women to challenge the debilitating social structures against their status. In the same way, the action of the wise virgins can teach African women to gather their children together to constantly wait upon the Lord and answer His summons whenever He calls.

The parables too have far more implications for the African church. In the parables, women are portrayed as agents of evangelization. As earlier observed they demonstrate qualities (i.e., patience, determination, faith, conviction, affection, etc.) which are characteristics of an evangelizer. In fact, it would appear that the parable of the Ten Virgins is only but a warning that success and failure are the lot of both men and women. The church must therefore enable women to develop their potentials through greater access to theological education. This would create for women rich avenues to unveil their potentials in the theological and missionary field and thereby make room for religious self-expression, self-awareness and self-actualization to their fullness.

Conclusion

The study has highlighted the fact that in the Bible some parables are designed to appeal primarily to men, others to women.

Thus, the message of the gospel is not meant for men alone but also for women. It is more significant that in the parables and other scenes dominated by female activities, Jesus raises up women as character models to portray clearly and vividly what God actually is. It is no wonder that in modern biblical hermeneutics true femininity is godliness. Hence, the attribute of the gifts of the Holy Spirit to the characters of women. Indeed, women's character of being loving, caring, preserving, enduring, etc., modeled by self-control are biblical gifts of the Holy Spirit which reveals the true nature of God as the third person of the most Holy Trinity.

Women today as in the parables are continuing to demonstrate those qualities that mark them as Godlike. The church must, therefore, look out for the lost coin vis-à-vis women long neglected, but well equipped with love, gentleness, and knowledge needed to reach millions of Christ's faithful, especially children, youths, and women themselves.

Notes

1. The book is advertised in *New Catholic World*, Vol. 216, No. 1292, Sept./Oct. 1973. Published by the Paulist Fathers.

2. Dorothea McEwan and Myra Poole "Making the Connections: The Global Agenda of Feminist Theology", *New Blackfriars*, Vol. 71, No. 838, May 1989, pp. 229-236.

3. Peter M.J. Stravinskas (ed.) *Our Sunday Visitor's Catholic Encyclopedia*, Indiana, p. 746.

4. Caroll Stuhlmueller (ed.) *The Collegeville Pastoral Dictionary of Biblical Theology*, Minnesota: The Liturgical Press, 1996, p. 689.

5. C.H. Dodd, *Parables of the Kingdom*, London: Collins Fontana Books, 1960, p. 16.

6. Stuhlmueller, *op.cit.*

7. Stravinskas, *op.cit.*

8. Joachim Jeremiah, *The Parables of Jesus*, London: SCM Press, 1972, p. 90.

9. Jeremiah, *Rediscovering the Parables*, N.V. Charles Scribner's Sons, 1996, p. 80.

10. See Stuhmueller, *op.cit.*, p. 691.

11. Rabbi Joshua B. Levi (first half of third century A.D.) said: "Great is Peace in the Earth as Leaven to dough; for had God not set peace on the earth, the sword and wild beast have depopulated it? See Edward A. Armstrong, *The Gospel Parables*, N.V. Sheed and Ward, 1967, p. 56.

12. The term Khamera in Syria dialect means dough. The root in Semitic language means ferment. Leaven in biblical times consisted of a piece of fermented dough from a previous baking.

13. Megan McKenna, *Not Counting Woman and Children*, N.V. Orbis Books, 1994, p. 747.

14 Pol Vonck, *Understanding 42 Parables*, Eldoret, AMECEA Gaba Pub., 1990, p. 28-29.

15. *Ibid.*

16. The NEB Translation which represents the Widow as "demanding justice" is more correct than the AV "avenge me of my adversary" as comparison of the language used in the Papyri has shown. "Adversary" is the usual word used for the opponent in a Lawsuit. Cr. J.H. Moulten and G. Milligan, *The Vocabulary of the New Testament*, 1906, p. 3.

17. Reginald H. Fuller, *Preaching the New Lectionary*, Minnesota: The Liturgical Press, 1974, p. 79.

18 Ibid.

19. William Barclay, The Daily Study Bible: The Gospel of Luke, Bangalore Theo. Pub., 1955, p. 22. Barclay's suggestions appears to be a moot point. Indeed, the Judge described as unjust is of a type that was all too common in Israel (cf. Am. 5:7, 10-13; Isa. 1:23, 5:7-23; Jer. 5:28).

20. Joseph Fichtner, *Many Things in Parables*, NY: Alba House, 1988, p. 96.

21 Fuller, *op.cit.*, p. 271.

22 Protus O. Kemdirim, "Oppression of Women and the Liberating Message of Jesus," *Journal of Inculturation Theology*, 1995, Vol. 2, No. 2, pp. 184-1985.

A Critical Review of Cheryl Exum's Feminist Interpretation of Hebrew Canon Patriarchy

Ramathate T.H. Dolamo

Introduction

This study looks at two publications by Exum, namely, *Fragmented Women* (1993) and *Plotted, Shot and Painted* (1996). It is my view that these books are a bedrock upon which Exum's hermeneutics is based, built and developed. She has, to my mind, developed a clear and convincing hermeneutical response to patriarchy in general in terms of its religion and culture. At the end of the review, fundamental questions are raised and some controversial statements made in order to engage us all in dialogue aimed at keeping issues of gender in a broader perspective.

Exum's Point of Departure

Exum's (1993) thesis is that the Bible is an androcentric document arising out of a patriarchal culture. As a result, most of the narratives in the Bible relate men's stories. The stories in which women *do* feature are generally fragmented and told in such a way that they serve only the interests of men and of the patriarchal culture. Using Freudian psychoanalytical tools, Exum subjects the stories of Jephthah's daughter, Michal, Manoah's wife, Samson's Timnite wife, the harlot of Gaza, Delilah, Sarah, Rebekah, Bathsheba and the Levite's unknown secondary wife (whom she calls Bathsheber) to feminist scrutiny. She shows how dutiful, submissive women are blessed with male children (Manoah's wife – chapter 3) and how the story of Jephthah's daughter teaches women to be submissive to the demands of patriarchal culture even though it may cost them their lives (chapter 1). Conversely, women who dare challenge patriarchal authority are cursed with 'barrenness' or the loss of their lives. So it is, for example, that Michal's womb is closed when she criticizes David's performance before the ark (chapter 1) and 'Bathsheber' is murdered through gang-rape. The latter suffers a violent death and her corpse is dismembered because, according to Exum, she incurred the male god's wrath by daring to flee from her Levite husband to Gibeath, in search of asylum from patriarchy. She propounds, on the basis of the narrative in which 'Bathsheber's story is told, that 'Bathsheber' is raped not only by the penis, but by the pen (chapter 6). A similar fate befalls Bathsheba who is taken by David against her will and is subsequently blamed for seducing him (chapter 6).

Exum (1996) entitled, *Plotted, Shot and Painted* is a follow-up on Exum's book entitled, *Fragmented Women* (1993) in that it still pursues studies in gender, culture and theory. Exum concentrates more on the question of gender bias in interpretation. The title of the book explains the purpose of the book, namely, to look into cultural representations of biblical women (plotted), to see how contemporary society has put biblical women on film (shot), and further to see how contemporary artists have interpreted biblical women's stories (painted).

Methods of Patriarchal Control

According to Exum (1993), pitting women against each other is one of the ways of maintaining patriarchal control over women's lives. In the case of Michal, the narrative pits Israelite women of different classes against each other (chapter 1). Furthermore, the narrative of Judges 13-16 pits Israelite and foreign women against each other. This narrative portrays Israelite women, represented by Manoah's wife, as submissive mothers, whilst foreign women – Samson's Timnite wife, the harlot of Gaza, and Delilah – are portrayed as being devious, sexually loose seductresses who make use of their sexuality to entice men (Samson) for their own ulterior motives (chapter 3). For her, these stories teach that women are not to be trusted, that female behaviour should be regulated by reward, and that women always "sell out" in patriarchy and thereby cooperate with (male) oppressors. They also teach that Israelite women are to be preferred above foreign women, even though the former may themselves have a 'bad' side. In other words, these stories serve specific gender interests, the main one being to control women and their sexuality, and to justify their subjugation.

Foreign women are not the only ones cast in a negative light, as the stories of Sarah, Rachel and Rebekah show. For, Sarah sends Hagar and her son, Ishmael, into the desert, and Rebekah initiates and completes Jacob's deception of Isaac in order to steal Esau's blessings (chapter 4). Furthermore, the voices of these matriarchs are heard only when their voices serve patriarchal concerns. For example, both Sarah and Rachel instruct their maidservants to mother a child for their respective husbands because they cannot do so themselves. The matriarchs in Genesis 12-35 are all barren – with the exception of Leah – until rescued by the patriarchal god. These stories show that patriarchy defines womanhood in terms of motherhood, and that the matriarchs are blessed as long as they stay within their patriarchally-determined confines. On the basis of this, Exum maintains that it is therefore important to understand the relations between patriarchy and matriarchy in terms of power relations (chapter 4).

Patriarchs and Matriarchs

Exum (1993) in chapter 6 draws our attention to patriarchal-matriarchal relations in showing us the extent to which the patriarchs were prepared to go in advancing their own causes at the expense of their wives as Genesis 12, 20, 26 narrate the stories.

In these chapters, we find three stories of God-fearing patriarchs who were willing to prostitute their wives in exchange for material benefits and their own safety. So it is that Sarah is taken up into Pharaoh and Abimelech's harems in Genesis 12 and 20 respectively, because Abraham tells the two men that she is his sister. Isaac does the same to his wife Rebekah, with the result that she is taken up into the harem of Abimelech of Gerar (Genesis 26). These women had no say in what happened to them. Exum applies Freudian psychoanalysis to understand the patriarch's unconscious fantasies and so to find a semiotic cure for their neurosis, the fear of women's sexuality underlying these three stories.

Exum's analysis of the stories mentioned above leads her to conclude that men fear women who are sexually independent and, as a result, the (male) narrators have established ways and means to control women and sanction those women who do not conform to phallocentric concerns. She uses very strong words against the patriarchs and men in general, including the narrators. She says, for example, that women – especially the matriarchs – are murdered and raped in the narratives and by the narratives. She also contends that, "Using class to divide women is a fundamental strategy of patriarchal ideology" (37).

Prophetic Pornography

Looking at "Prophetic Pornography" in chapter 4, Exum (1996) makes a selection of texts in the Hebrew Canon to prove the extent to which men would go to oppress, ridicule, rape, murder and dismember women in the name of YHWH. These shocking and scandalizing texts have even been toned down in most translations. Hosea (1-3) makes use of husband-wife metaphor for God's relation to God's people and denigrates women by referring to them as whores and prostitutes. Isaiah (1:21, 57:3-13) calls Jerusalem a harlot and the language of sexual humiliation of women is also used. Jeremiah (2:23-24) follows suit when he refers to Israel's unfaithfulness in terms of illicit female sexual activity and woman is caricatured as a young camel or wild donkey in heat. Ezekiel uses the strongest and most abusive language. Jerusalem is depicted as a whore before whom God would bring all her lovers to see her nudity after which they would be given turns to abuse and rape her (16:35-38). The most pornographic example is found in Ezekiel 23. In Lamentations (1:8-10), we find a woman who is coopted and she is made to blame herself because of her sexual unfaithfulness.

Exum concludes this chapter by suggesting four ways of addressing these biblical texts in which the deity violently abuse a nation, metaphorically cast as a woman. Firstly, attention should be given to the differing claims these texts make upon their male and female readers; secondly, prophetic pornography should be exposed for what it is; thirdly, competing discourses should be identified especially where women's voices are suppressed and female experiences are denied or misnamed and lastly, that a systematic deconstructive reading of the texts in question should deliberately be undertaken.

Women Stories

In chapter 3, "The Hand That Rocks The Cradle," Exum (1996) gives an account of a story about reading and re-reading the account of Moses' birth in which women play a pivotal role. Exum examines Exodus 1-2 in a vain attempt to salvage some texts that put women in a favorable light. But she realizes that these women are only useful for the narrators to the extent that the baby Moses is saved, nurtured and raised. Once he is a grown man, his mother, sister

Miriam, Pharaoh's daughter and the midwives disappear from the scene and are forgotten.

Exum (88) cautions as follows:

> If we read according to the ideology of the text available to us in the surface structure, and stop there, we are left with the ancient (male) authors' views of women, which, in the case of Exodus 1-2, happen to be affirmative. But to see how the positive portrayal of women in Exod. 1:8-2:10 nevertheless serves male interests, we need to interrogate the ideology that motivates it. Granted that women are given important roles here, we need to ask, what androcentric interests does this positive presentation promote?

She therefore recommends that feminist critics should step outside the ideology of the text and understand women in the biblical literature as male constructs; and in order to maintain and perpetuate itself, patriarchy depends on women's complicity. Force, threat and fear are often used to ensure that women comply. But the greatest and most effective weapon men use, according to Exum, is to reward women who comply and cooperate with men in their own oppression and exploitation. Exum regards with suspicion phrases such as "the hand that rocks the cradle rules the world" and "behind every great man is a woman" because such phrases tell women indirectly and politely that they should stay within the confines of the domestic sphere and motherhood and leave the public arena to men.

Whilst women are relegated to the background from Exodus 4 onwards, men tend to even appropriate some of women's capabilities of birth and nurturing. For example, it is a (male) God who makes women barren or fertile, and in Numbers 11, Moses complains to God that it was not him who gave birth to Israel that they should ask for food and shelter from him.

Women on Film and on Canvas

Bathsheba

Chapter 1 of Exum (1996) deals with Bathsheba as the object of the male gaze as objectified by the narrative, painting and film. But more importantly is the fact that, against their own interests, women are also coopted in these presentations of the naked woman. In chapter 6 entitled "Raped by the Pen," Exum (1993) does speak of physical and sexual violence of Bathsheba by David. But Exum goes on to show that Bathsheba was also metaphorically raped by the biblical male narrator, by portraying David in a favourable light whilst Bathsheba is portrayed as a seductress, though she was having a bath in the privacy of her bathroom. According to Exum (1996), both the 1951 film, "David and Bathsheba" and the 1985 "King David" shows the same depiction of Bathsheba as a temptress. Bathsheba's beauty is held against her by the narrator, and subsequent representations in paintings and films accept the concept of woman as a source of temptation that can bring about a man's downfall.

The story of David and Bathsheba has provided an artistic representation of a naked woman according to Exum. She indicates further that the paintings carry associations of shame, sin and guilt. A painting of Bathsheba by Rembrandt, "Bethsabie au bain" has however a redeeming feature in that she is not an exhibitionist; her head is turned away indicating her reluctance to be seen according to Exum's observation. After examining other paintings such as Hans Memlings' 15th century painting, the Dutch artist, Cornelis Cornelisz van Haarlem's (1562-1638), the 17th century painting by Carlo Maratti and the early 17th century painting by Hans van Aachen, she comes to one conclusion viz, that Bathsheba is accused of vanity and consequently she is being held responsible for her fate.

Film is by nature a voyeuristic medium according to Exum. The cinematic Bathsheba is obviously guided by the lens. We can gaze only at what the camera chooses to show us. In the 1951 film,

"David and Bathsheba," we are put in David's position, men and women alike. We are shown David's arousal that activates his lustful gaze. The "King David" film uses more lighting than the earlier one to create a mood of sensuality. The whole atmosphere exudes sensuousness and concupiscence. Exum commends the 1980s production because it leaves less of the erotic to the imagination. While watching the film, Exum picks another dimension, a lesbian relationship. She observes that Bathsheba's attendant runs her hands over her body and her breasts thoroughly. Indeed, there are suggestions of homo-eroticism and nymphomania, certainly not innocent washing, in the way Bathsheba enjoys her bath.

Exum concludes that the plot, film and painting of Bathsheba are in cahoots in trying to frame her while David goes free and guiltless, even though David took Uriah's wife and had him killed in battle. David's punishment for adultery is that his wives would be raped. What did the two women do to deserve to be raped as punishment for their husband's sin? Exum would like to have a rational and logical explanation.

Michal

Chapter 2 of Exum (1996) is entitled, "Michal at the Window, Michal in the Movies." The plot is played out in Exum (1993:11ff). She is a nagging wife who arrogantly defies both her father Saul and husband David. Michal is on a war path with patriarchy in general and she is consequently punished by the (male) God with barrenness and sexual neglect and deprivation by her husband.

Films on Michal make do with cinematic gap-filling in their attempts at interpreting the biblical story. True to the biblical account, the film, "David and Bathsheba" does not mention David's love for Michal but Michal loved David. It seems that David was only concerned with using his marriage to Michal as a stepping stone to Saul's throne. But the situation is reversed in "King David" in that David loves her, but she spurns him in order to return to her second husband. Michal quarrels with David in the two films only once, when David dances denuded before the Ark (2 Sam. 6). It seems her emotional outburst is due to sexual jealousy. Both films portray Michal in an unfavourable light. She is to blame for everything that goes wrong, including her being wronged by David.

Naomi

"Is this Naomi?" the title of chapter 5 in Exum (1996), is a question prompted by a painting by Philip Hermogenes Calderon (1883-1898) of two people in an embrace. Is it Ruth and Naomi? Are they really two women in an embrace? But it is so erotic that if they both are women, then the relationship could be construed as lesbianism (Ruth 1:16-17). But then could the other person who is older and more masculine be Boaz? Of course, to ask such questions one needs to have the biblical knowledge about the picture. Exum believes that same and opposite relationships are both discernable in the story and in the painting. However, the strength of the relationship that exists between Naomi and Ruth is weakened when Boaz comes into the picture. Naomi's center stage in Ruth's life is taken by Boaz. According to Exum (144), "The book of Ruth is not a story about how two women make a life together in a man's world, but a story about the continuity of a family, and this requires the presence of a man."

The 1960 film "The Story of Ruth" makes Naomi old enough to be Boaz's mother and the affection between the two women is toned down and any suggestion of erotic feelings on the part of either woman is eliminated. Many paintings make Naomi a really old, haggard and care-worn woman such as, for example, William Blake's "Naomi and Her Two Daughters-in-Law," Thomas Matthew Rooks' 19th century painting and Pieter Lastman's "Ruth Swears Loyalty to Naomi" (1614). "The Story of Ruth," a 1960 Hollywood film, turns the story into a love story – a heterosexual love story.

Delilah

"Why, Why, Why, Delilah," the title of chapter 6 in Exum (1996), ". . . is about a woman who betrays her lover with another man and then adds insult to injury by laughing at him when he confronts her" (176).

In the 1949 film, "Samson and Delilah," Samson says Delilah would be cursed on the lips of men as punishment for her betrayal. Over the years, Delilah has been regarded as a problem to men. She is regarded as a temptress. She is treacherous, sexually irresistible, at once both fascinating and frightening and ultimately deadly. She is regarded as *"femme fatale,"* the woman fatal to men. Exum points out that the entire biblical story of Samson and Delilah consists of a mere 18 verses, and just over 300 words in the Hebrew. And yet the actions of this minor character, Delilah, had serious consequences for the Israelites and the Philistines. Relatively very little is known about her. Was she a Philistine or an Israelite? Was she a propertied widow like Judith or was she a harlot made rich by her trade? This story portrays a seductive woman who schemes and plots to destroy Samson and, as usual with biblical stories, she disappears as soon as the mission is accomplished.

Exum notices a familiar trend whereby male narrators divide women into good and bad, that is, ". . . the woman on the pedestal who is venerated (the virgin, the mother) and the whore, the fallen woman, the woman to be scorned and looked down on" (186). For example, Samson's mother is wife and mother and she knows her place and does not challenge patriarchal authority (Judges 13). The other woman, Delilah, is bad and uses her sexual charms and attractions to lead Samson astray. Women are also divided along ethnic lines. Israelite men should not have relations with foreign women such as the Philistines, for they are inherently evil and religiously unclean. Proverbs (2:18-19) warns Israelite men against marrying from other tribes.

Western art perpetrates the contemporary image of Delilah as a prostitute. The Oxford English Dictionary describes Delilah in similar negative sexual connotations for example. Gustave Moreau's painting portrays the woman's body as a signifier of male desire.

Her voluptuousness accounts for Samson's inability to resist. Peter Paul Rubens' painting, "Samson and Delilah," also depicts Delilah as a prostitute and in another painting by the same person, Delilah is again depicted as a prostitute. Whichever way the story is told, women are represented in a way that they are denigrated and abused.

Conclusion

These books are a must for all men in every culture, especially black African males whose culture is very similar to the biblical culture, particularly that of the Hebrew Canon. They also hold a very important lesson for women, namely, that they should not allow themselves to be divided along the lines of race, ethnicity, religious affiliation, and class. Women must engender gender solidarity among themselves if they are to liberate themselves from male bondage. In this way, they may contribute meaningfully toward nation-building by eliminating gender bondage. It would also not be useful for women to discard the Bible or certain portions of it in the quest for a Bible that is free from androcentrism, but rather appropriate such tools as provided by Exum among other scholars. One may also say, in the same breath, that men should not close their eyes to women being blatantly and nakedly abused in the Bible in the name of YHWH. We need a methodology, acceptable to men and women, whose intention would be to restore the God-given human dignity offered to the human race by Godself.

One would like to make the following blunt and provocative statements:

Firstly, women have been made scapegoats since the beginning of the world. It was Eve who introduced sin in the world. She made an attempt to pass on the blame to the snake without much success, and, through the biblical times until today, as Exum so aptly shows, women are blamed for almost everything that goes wrong.

Secondly, women have been and are still blamed for what they are in terms of gender or sex. They are manipulators who will do anything to get what they want. Thus Delilah uses all her sexual charms to lure Samson into a trap. Even where women do not actively seduce men, they are blamed for being "beautiful" or for being generously endowed. Thus Bathsheba having a bath in private is being surreptitiously watched by David and she ends up being blamed for tempting David into raping her.

Thirdly, women have allowed themselves to be coopted into their own oppression and exploitation by submitting to divisions along ethnic, religious, and class lines. Thus, Sarah abuses Hagar to please Abraham, and Samson's mother is held in high esteem at the expense of Delilah.

Fourthly, as Exum shows, nothing much has changed for women since the biblical times. The contemporary society still perpetuates patriarchal values and norms that disallow women's emancipation. Paintings and films today still portray women as objects of male gaze and abuse. Women's bodies are being used in advertisements and in pornography and their lack of financial independence is being exploited to the full.

Fifthly, women are their worst enemies. Patriarchy has put them in a strategic position in which they could teach their children only the liberating aspects of culture, but sadly, that opportunity is more often than not, allowed to slip. Women do sometimes pull one another down instead of supporting and encouraging one another. Men do sometimes succeed in dividing women.

What is the purpose of these statements? Women should realize that they are the only people who can liberate themselves from patriarchy and the contemporary culture, notwithstanding some few men who are genuinely interested in their emancipation. As the slogan goes, power is not given but it is seized. Gender in terms of male and female category is a power relations exercise. Women should unite in order to fight together the struggle against male domination in family, church, and society at large.

Bibliography

Exum, J.C. 1993. *Fragmented Women: Feminist (Sub)versions of Biblical Narratives.* Valley Forge, U.S.A: Press International.

Exum, J.C. 1996. *Plotted, Shot, and Painted: Cultural Representations of Biblical Women.* England: Sheffield Academic Press.

Gender Mainstreaming In African Theology
An African Woman's Perspective

Philomena N. Mwaura

Introduction

Gender as a category of analysis is gaining acceptance and has now been included in many disciplines such as economics, philosophy, political science, psychology, literature and education. Just as in the 1970s and 1980s, liberation theology recognized that socio-economic and racial-ethnic identity influences the theological task, so too have liberation theologians realized in the 1990s that gender as a social construct plays a significant role in their presuppositions, attitudes and the way in which they focus on their object of study. However, whereas economic and racial injustice have been exposed and denounced vehemently by both men and women, sexism has received mixed reactions. Although for example feminist theology has been an issue in EATWOT since 1981, there has never been a real dialogue between men and women "about feminist critiques of patriarchy in Christian theologians."[1]

This theological unwillingness to deal with women's issues and concerns is also present in African Liberation Theology. While it exposes and analyzes social-economic and political oppression, colonial and neo-colonial, it has not adequately addressed gender based oppression. Sexism is even sanctioned in the name of cultural traditions. However, as Mercy Oduyoye observes:

> African men theologians are beginning to own up to the reality that African women have unveiled (injustice). Few will however admit to their privileged position derived from their being men, and few seem to be reading what African women theologians write.[2]

She goes on to identify the obstacles that hinder effective gender dialogue within EATWOT as:

> first, "men's traditional fear of women; and women who fear conflict have joined together to prevent dialogue from taking place,"

> secondly, "men would not touch what they hear as threatening. Sharing personal experience as a starting point for theologizing threatens men. Subjects that state the oppression of women are heard by men as an attempt to send them on a guilt trip..."[3]

These observations aptly describe the situation of theological reflection on women concerns within EATWOT particularly in the Kenyan context. During the EATWOT Theological Commission Conference (Kenya chapter) in 1998, members of the Women's Commission presented papers on a variety of issues focusing on the Commission theme "Women for a New World Order: Response of Third World Women Theologians."

Out of twenty-five papers, about nine papers were presented by women. By the end of the last presentation, there were very many complaints and murmurings from the men colleagues to the effect that "our women are not oppressed," "you have borrowed a foreign ideology and imposed it on our women"; and "this is just a problem of disgruntled educated, western oriented women." These comments and attitudes masked the real issues of equity, equality, liberation and oppression on account of gender, ethnicity or class. They hindered dialogue and men and women seemed to adopt opposing positions. This situation continues to repeat itself in other theological deliberations.

It is true as noted that EATWOT has encouraged gender dialogue. Some African men theologians like Charles Nyamiti[4], Simon Maimela[5], Emmanuel Martely[6], and Tinyiko Maluleke[7] have even taken gender seriously in their theologizing. However, African women theologians are not satisfied with the way gender has been addressed by African theology. Mercy Oduyoye, for example, charges that most of Africa's progressive theological "traditions, inculturationist, liberationist, translationist, and reconstructionist are nothing but 'smokescreens' from under which Western Christian patriarchy and African Christian patriarchy engage in a combined offensive against African women."[8]

- What are the obstacles towards gender dialogue in African theology?
- Why do women have to address their concerns and conditions of marginalization alone while these conditions are not self-created?
- What is gender in relation to theology?
- Is failure to achieve gender dialogue related to lack of understanding of the term?
- How can gender be mainstreamed in theology?
- How can gender practice and perspective effect the language and images of the divine in the African context?

These are the questions that this paper seeks to address. It will begin by giving an operational definition of gender, examine what has been happening in the Kenyan context and then reflect on how gender practice and perspective may enlighten and affect our language and images of God.

What is Gender?

Gender is an analytical concept that refers to a system of roles and relationships between men and women, that are determined not by biology, but by the social, political and economic context. It is different from sex, which is a biological category which identifies the biological differences between men and women. Gender, therefore, refers not simply to women or men, but to the relationship between them, and the way it is socially constructed. Because it is a relational term, it must include men and women.

Traditionally, society assumes that there are observable differences between the sexes but it is known that personality, behaviour and abilities are the result of differential socialization. A working definition of gender is that people are born female and male, but learn to be girls and boys who grow into women and men. They are taught what the appropriate behaviour and attitudes, roles and activities are for them, and how they should relate to other people. This learned behaviour makes up gender identity and determines gender roles. Gender identity evolves throughout childhood and during adulthood. The construction of gender roles and relationships is a permanent process. Parents and siblings, relatives and friends all play a part in reinforcing certain behaviours for boys and girls while discouraging others. School plays a formative role as do the media, and other institutions like religion that transmit values, role models and stereotypes.[9]

Gender roles, which are the determined patterns of behaviour in terms of rights, duties, obligations, and prerogatives assigned to females and males in society, are not universal. They differ from one society to another, from place to place and over time. They also differ according to race, class and even age. Gender roles are maintained and reinforced through the same processes of learning. Society's perception and attitudes towards gender roles, responsibilities and their worth are often based on value judgement and stereotyping. Religion plays a significant part in maintaining and legitimizing roles, attitudes and perceptions of the various genders through beliefs, teachings, ritual, language, etc. In the African context, this has adverse consequences on the lives and status of women.

In Kenya for example, the social organization of most pre-colonial and present day communities is patriarchal and patrilocal. Gender asymmetry is a significant feature. The patriarchal ideology has different and even adverse implications for women and their status compared to men. Patriarchy legitimizes the subordination of women who experience themselves as persons primarily in relation to others – as mother or wife. A woman's social status usually depends on these relationships and not on any qualities or achievements of her own.

Despite modern education and advances made by women in the social, political and economic spheres, this kind of thinking still prevails. In some quarters, boy children are still valued over girl children. Women today, just like in pre-colonial communities, are overtly excluded from power and hence decision making processes due to their gender. Patriarchal structures are supported by a culture which gives rational explanation for this exclusion of women and dominance by men. The consequence of these gender asymmetries in terms of roles, perception and status accorded to women as person is:

- Inequalities along gender lines.
- Non-participation of women in leadership.
- Unequal gender power relations.
- Inculcation of feelings of inferiority within the girl child, older girls and women.
- Apathy in women leading to few women aspiring to leadership positions in church and society.

- Women's occupation of low decision making positions: Women for example, making decisions about food, subsistence farming and other non-monetary matters. In the church they are confined to diakonia ministries, fund raising, teaching catechism to children, decorating and cleaning churches. Men on the other hand make decisions about the family resources, etc. In the church, men dominate leadership, theology, and make decisions regarding its life and activities.
- Low self-esteem.
- Poverty and lack of economic empowerment..
- Women's lack of legal and human rights.
- Girls' and women's inadequate access to education; poor performance and failure to complete their education due to negative cultural attitudes that favour boys and men over girls and women.[10]

African women theologians concur that culture is the arena of African women's oppression. According to Musimbi,[11] Edet,[12] and Oduyoye,[13] culture is to African women's liberation theology what race relations are to African American theologians. This is not to say that there are no other structures that are oppressive to women. But gender, class and ethnicity in Africa are all tied up with culture, if we take culture as a concept to cover among other things, marriage, organization of family systems or parenthood, social class, religion, trade, government and language. Culture as such consists of habits that are shared by members of a society. The sharing may be general throughout the society as in the case of language, or it may be limited to particular categories of people within society, for example by gender, age group, social class, associations, or occupational groups.

African culture embodies certain practices that dehumanize women. It socializes them to be submissive, unassuming and tolerant. These are dispositions that can be oppressive and African women have not adequately voiced their experiences of injustices.

Culture has silenced and hindered them from experiencing the liberating promises of God. Some aspects of our cultures which diminish women are embraced without considering their oppressive nature. In Kenya, for instance, practices like clitoridectomy, infibulation, early marriages, widowhood rites, food and relationship taboos are still widely practiced and are yet to be eradicated. Their continuance finds support among both men and women.

The family as the nucleus of society and the scene where culture is preserved has the potential of either being liberating to women or engendering their subordination. Although it has been a center of support for both men and women, it has reinforced gender stereotypes and perpetuated the *status quo*.

Heterogeneity within Africa

But who are the women we describe as oppressed by culture in the African context? The nature of women's condition in Africa as elsewhere is multi-various. Their roles, needs and problems may differ by region, ethnic group, social economic status, religion and culture. There are also many different groups among women who may be vulnerable and disadvantaged. Some of these vulnerable and special groups include the girl child, female heads of households, adolescent mothers, the rural urban poor and illiterate. It would therefore be a mistake to generalize on the situation and the roles of the Kenyan woman if one takes into consideration the heterogeneous nature of the society. Nevertheless, regardless of the social class and the fact that some women by virtue of social class or ethnicity may hold a status of privilege, domination and oppression, women in all patriarchal cultures are perceived to have inferior status compared to men.

This heterogeneity or difference should not become a source of fear, bias, and ignorance that results in injustice. But it can also be a platform for trying to understand the differences and for celebrating variety.

The Task of African Women Theologians

This context is the experience of women in Africa and it is the one that women theologians are analyzing and exposing with its inherent gender injustice. This injustice is compounded by appropriation of the biblical histories, which are rooted in patriarchy and is part of the biblical cultural heritage (both Jewish and Greco-Roman). This, too, is our own heritage. Women's theological reflection has shown how patriarchy has affected our experience and naming of God. Patriarchy has shaped our structures of work, worship and decision making. These theologians (feminist/womanist) name the gender injustices that women experience globally. While women's theologies appeal to solidarity to combat the subordination of women, they also include the concerns of women affected by social injustice such as racism, poverty, culture, etc. Hence, they address the concerns of the different categories of women that we have identified.

Gender analysis by women theologians (feminist/womanist) has attempted to analyze critically the conceptual processes which generate, nurture and maintain engendered characteristics of society. It looks for clues in human language, culture, social structures, symbolic representation and folk traditions.

African women theologians have the task of not only critiquing culture but reclaiming the theological heritage stored in the participation of African women in traditional religion. Although Oduyoye[14] does not support the view that women were prominent in traditional cults, in West Africa, Phiri in her work on the Chewa shows that religious leadership and sometimes secular, was in the hands of women as prophetesses at rain shrines.[15] Women in most African communities were also priestesses, mediums, diviners, healers and media persons. Their gifts were divinely endowed and meant for the service of the community.

In addition, the African institutional churches are providing structures within which women may acquire power, responsibility and hence serve the community of God. Although their functions are also inhibited by a number of stringent taboos, there are avenues of participation in mediating God's love and building the church. But gender stereotyping still remains within the church whether mainline or African instituted. What is the task of theology in eliminating stereotypes and building an inclusive community?

Reflection on Gender Practices

We have observed that in order to build a community of faith where both men and women are actually seen to reflect the image of God, and a community characterized by love, justice and equality, a gender perspective is a must in doing theology as well as in the faith and practice of the church. Women's concerns, out of which their theology arises, should not be peripheral but central. As Ada Maria Diaz aptly puts it:

> It is not enough to be satisfied with the number of women doing theology, but the question is, how are women issues dealt with? What difference does our concerns make to the process of theologizing? Gender analysis has been ignored or made peripheral.[16]

Another woman, Christine Grumm, calls for mainstreaming of a gender perspective in all church planning, programming and implementation, for focusing on so called women's concerns leading to marginalization of women. To her, there are no women's issues but community ones, for they all impact in one way or other on both men and women.[17]

We agree with this observation and argue that gender mainstreaming should be a perspective in theologizing. By this we mean using a gender lens to examine the total work of the church in mission, diakonia and proclamation. There are gender issues in liturgy, our conception of God, Christology, the Trinity, the language of theology, or describing the God-head, development projects and programmes, leadership participation, the interpretation and teaching of the Bible and, indeed, the whole process of doing theology.

Our gender practice and perspective, for example, affect the way we conceive God and talk about God. The very idea of thinking about God in an inclusive manner other than male, in Africa today, arouses passionate feelings. Church people, and even those who consider themselves liberals and have accepted inclusive language in other fields, exhibit phobic reactions to the possibility of speaking of God as a "she." One woman pastor was recently demoted and denied further theological training for daring to address God in a communal prayer as "Father-Mother-God."[18] This hostility arises much more out of the Judeo-Christian formation of the normative image of God as male. However, in our African traditional religion, God has attributes that evoke feminine characteristics. In fact, African myths of origin have images of women which leads one to conclude that African religion is less sexist in its image of God than other religions. The female images of God have made it possible for women to perform priestly functions in the worship of the deity and of his functionaries who are of both sexes.[19] The African concept of God is not altogether masculine. In fact, some communities like the Gikuyu and Chewa believe that God is neither male nor female. God has neutral gender and embodies in "itself" the attributes of both.

God is a power, a spirit, and yet has anthropomorphic characteristics. As such, he/she is compassionate and gentle with creation "like a sheep without horns."[20] God is also the originator of life, a function attributed to female deities for example among the Yoruba. The Yoruba, too, conceive the creator as a female. It is only with regard to her/his association with leadership and strength that later traditions transformed her into a male deity. From the myths, we can deduce that even in African religion, the equality of human beings as male and female is embedded in the divine ordering of things just like in the Genesis creation story. The dominance of the solely patriarchal image of God can be attributed to human creation in its development of culture. Gendered roles and perspectives have been confounded by patriarchy which according to feminist and gender theories also arose within history but not in God's design for his/her creation. Unless the sin of patriarchy as a system of power is confessed to and challenged in and by theology, church and society, there can be no gender justice particularly for women.

Religions including Christianity have supported patriarchy. Patriarchy also engenders the perpetration of violence against women. Christianity and even African religion have had a history of misogyny. However, it is comforting to know from our discussion on gender that gender is not permanent or God ordained. Since it is socially and historically constructed, it can be deconstructed and reconstructed, based on new foundations and criteria.

In the Bible, the male patriarchal images of God are depicted as too limited to represent the variety of relationships of God to Israel. In certain texts, God is described as a mother, a woman in travail. These images occur periodically when God's unconditional love and faithfulness to the people of Israel, despite their sins, is described. God is compassionate, forgiving, and seeks to bring Israel to a new birth of repentance (cf. Isaiah 41:13-14; 16-17). In the wisdom tradition, the female image appears as a second person of God mediating the work and will of God. Rosemary Reuther says, "behind this powerful image of wisdom lies the goddess who was traditionally characterized as wisdom, but in Hebrew thought she has become a dependent attribute, an expression of the transcendent male God rather than an autonomous female manifestation of the divine.[21]

The point to be noted is that humanity has always conceived God as male and female. The feminine images of God have been conveniently overlooked. Hence, as Marianne Katopo remarks, the texts that have come to us are "products of a society driven to choose male metaphors by virtue of patriarchal structures predicated upon sexual inequality."[22] Again, in Christian tradition, particularly the early texts, the spirit is referred to as female and hence as Reuther says, "we cannot conclude that female imagery of the spirit is a later deviation of heretical Christianity."[23]

To achieve inclusiveness, it is important to conceive and name God in female as well as male metaphors. The image we in Africa have of God from 'his' representation in pictures (iconography) is a white old man with a long, white beard. He is also depicted as loving and ruthless. Hence, it is an uphill task convincing people otherwise.

However, inculturation theology and its implementation in the churches is contributing towards challenging this perspective; but God still remains male. This gendered perspective can only be challenged and changed through the re-reading and re-interpretation of the Bible from an African and African woman's perspective. There is need to create awareness of a liberative Christology. For women, Jesus is a role model because He is a fighter for justice, a healer and a teacher. They feel affirmed and encouraged when they see Jesus calling them to resist being overwhelmed by the injustice they face. This affirmation they see in the resurrected Christ is not related to Jesus being male. What the women relate to is his being God – loving, caring, and compassionate. However, single mothers do confess too that Jesus is their "husband." This is not conceived in a functional sense but ontologically.

The stories in the Bible, both Old and New Testaments (particularly Jesus' encounter with women), show a radical departure from the Jewish patriarchal culture, regarding women. God is depicted in the Bible as not the creator or validator of existing hierarchical and oppressive social order, but one who liberates us from it, the one who opens up a community of equals where there is "no slave, nor free, no Jew or Gentile, but all are one in Christ Jesus."[24] The Bible is both liberating and a supporter of oppression.

However, using it for liberation means claiming for ourselves and identifying what is part of the Jewish patriarchal culture and is oppressive, and was meant for a particular group and adopting what is universal and liberating. As Musimbi argues: "Women will need to sincerely claim biblical liberation without being apologetic to the culture set-up in which the message of the biblical passage has found its audience today.[25]

Conclusion

Doing theology from a gender perspective in Africa therefore calls for the ability to hear and embrace the good news of the Kingdom of God through which poverty, discrimination, gender based economic and political injustices, unemployment, religious oppression and inequalities are challenged. The church has a pastoral responsibility to both men and women, but focus should be more on women in order to elevate them from their marginal conditions. Ecclesiastical language should continually be challenged despite the existing hostility. For women to be empowered, language which employs images that evoke a power structure hierarchically structured (e.g., God, men, women, etc.) needs to be changed. Genesis 1:27 depicts an androgynous image of God, both male and female.

Male language for the divine should lose its privilege. The names for God should be taken as symbolic or analogy but not as describing biological attributes of God. God being male and female goes beyond human limited conceptions of who God is. We conclude by reiterating that gender is socially constructed and is therefore variable and can be reconstructed. Remaining on a particular frame of thinking or operating about God, negates the dynamic nature of human potentiality and culture. It also impoverishes our conception of the divine and the way we appropriate it. The church should recognize sexism as an evil and give it the same sanction it has given to issues of social-economic injustice and race. It should be a community of equals where gender hierarchies and oppression have no place. Theology on gender concerns should also be a task for both men and women and not women alone. Women's or men's concerns are the concerns of everybody.

Notes

1. Ivone Gebara, "A historical perspective from a Latin American viewpoint", *Voices from the Third World*, XIX, No. 1, June 1996, p. 41.

2. Mercy Amba Oduyoye, *Voices*, XIX, No. 1, June 1996, p. 20.

3. *Ibid.*, p. 28.

4. Charles Nyamiti, "The African Sense of God's Motherhood in Light of Christian Faith," *Voices*, Vol. 8, September 1985.

5. Simon Maimela, *Voices*, XIX, No. 1, June 1996.

6. Emmanuel Martely, "Women and Culture in Contemporary Africa" in Kemdirim Protus (ed.) *Women, Culture and Theological Education*, Enugu: West Africa Association of Theological Institutions, 1998, pp. 38-65.

7. Tinyiko Maluleke, "Reflecting Jesus Christ Crucified and Living Among Africa's Cross Bearers" unpublished paper presented at the International Association for Mission Studies Conference, Hamanskraal, South Africa, January 2000.

8. Mercy Amba Oduyoye, *Daughters of Anowa: African Women and Patriarchy*, New York: Orbis Books, 1995, pp. 180-181.

9. Economic Commission for Africa: Gender and Gender Mainstreaming, Addis Ababa, 1997.

10. Philomena N. Mwaura, "Empowerment of Women: The Role of Church", *Journal of African Christian Thought*, Vol. 1, No. 1, June 1998, p. 29.

11. Musimbi Kanyoro, *In Search of a Round Table: Gender, Theology and the Church*, Geneva: World Council of Churches, 1997, p. 30.

12. Rosemary Edet, "Men and Women Building the Church in Africa, *Voices*, Vol. 8, September 1985.

13. Mercy Amba Oduyoye, *Hearing and Knowing: The Theological Reflections of Christianity in Africa*, New York: Orbis Books.

14. *Ibid.*, p. 123.

15. Isabel Phiri, *Women, Presbyterianism and Patriarchy: Religious Experiences of Chewa Women in Malawi*, Blantyre: Kachere Books.

16. Ada Maria Diaz, "The Present and Future of EATWOT", *Voices*, XIX, June 1, 1996.

17. Christine Grumm, "In Search of a Round Table", in Kanyoro (ed.) *In Search*

of a Round Table, Gender Theology and the Church, New York: Orbis Books, p. 30.

18. This happened to a woman pastor in one of the mainline Protestant churches in Kenya.

19. Joseph Akinyele Omoyajowo, "The Role of Women in African Traditional Religion and Among the Yoruba", in J. Olupona (ed.) *African Traditional Religions in Contemporary Society*, New York: Paragon House, 1991, pp. 75-76.

20. The Gikuyu of Central Kenya describe God in this way.

21. Rosemary Radford Reuther, *Sexism and God Talk*, London: SCM, 1983, p. 57.

22. Marianne Katapo, "Perspectives for a Women's Theology:, *Voices*, Vol. 8, September 1983, p. 29.

23. Reuther, *op.cit.*, p. 59.

24. Galations 3:16, *The Holy Bible, Revised Standard Version*, 1971.

25. Musimbi Kanyoro, "Bible Studies at the Convocation", in Mercy Oduyoye *Talitha Quimi! Proceedings of the Convocation of African Women Theologians*, Ibadan: Dayster, pp. 52-53.

www.ingramcontent.com/pod-product-compliance
Lightning Source LLC
Chambersburg PA
CBHW070917180426
43192CB00038B/1739